TABLE OF CONTENTS

Dedication i
Foreword by JOHN A. HARDON, SJ iv

One
THE SON OF GOD 2000 I

Two
GOD OUR LOVING FATHER 13

Three
THE GOD OF HOLINESS 25

Four
THE GOD OF THE KINGDOM 37

Five
THE GOD WHO RULES 51

Six
THE GOD WHO PROVIDES 67

Seven
THE GOD WHO FORGIVES 83

Eight
THE GOD WHO DELIVERS US 101

Nine
MOTHER OF GOD 2000 119

FOREWORD

Of the scores of books I have been asked to review over the years of my priesthood, one of the most fascinating, I can honestly say, is **GOD 2000** by Fr. Richard Foley, a fellow-Jesuit based in London. What he writes in this excellent book makes it essential reading for us at the outset of the 21st century and the dawn of the third millennium. For it serves as a wonderful spiritual preparation, presenting us with a broad picture of what the Catholic faith tells us about the God of time and eternity, the God of human destiny.

Now a synthesis of our faith can be constructed from the principal ways whereby God places himself at the service of his children. And these ways happen to be expressed with marvellous precision and clarity in the Lord's Prayer. Very aptly, then, Fr. Foley uses its seven petitions as the framework of his book.

As with everything Jesus said and did, there is always more to it than appears at first glance. And this certainly applies to the Our Father prayer he gave his followers. Its numerous aspects have been expounded down the centuries by many spiritual writers, including such masters as St. Thomas Aquinas. **GOD 2000** comes as a welcome addition to the Church's vast library of theological and spiritual literature on the subject, and deserves to be read in every Catholic household.

In his final chapter the author outlines in loving detail the pivotal place and role of the Mother of God 2000 in the life of the Church---and, no less, in our personal lives---as we enter the new millennium. Nor should we enter it afraid, since God our providential Creator loves us infinitely, only asking of us in return that we love him with everything we have.

There are no shortcuts to holiness. We must know our faith in order to live our lives fully as Christians. Nor can we give others what we do not have ourselves. Readers will find much in this book to help them not only understand their faith better but, as opportunity allows, to share it with non-Catholics as well as with those who have fallen away.

Fr. Foley is doing the Church and the faithful a wonderful service through this work. Indeed, as was also the case with his most recent **MARY AND THE EUCHARIST**, I cannot recommend his newest book highly enough.

Fr. John A. Hardon, SJ
Detroit, Mi.
January 1, 2000

Chapter ONE

SON OF GOD 2000

There was a dramatic sense of occasion when the clocks chimed that final midnight and the year 2000 was ushered into our lives, bringing with it not only a brand-new century but a freshly-minted millennium. And because the 20th century's departure was also a farewell occasion of a special kind, it was heavy with nostalgia and *Auld Lang Syne*. Indeed, it was like saying goodbye to an old friend that had been part of our lives. Along with it the second millennium too disappeared over time's horizon and now rests in the graveyard of history.

Meanwhile, however, these momentous calendar changes notwithstanding, life goes on very much as usual. For "time takes no holidays," as an old proverb reminds us. Only at an Alice in Wonderland tea-party could time conceivably stand still. But in the real world it is constantly on the move, unstoppably so, and we have no option but to move along with it. As a wise man has pointed out, life must be lived forward though it can only be understood backward.

So 2000 is now with us, hurtling its way second by second into the unknown future. But we can and do face that future unafraid, full of confidence and optimism. For we possess God's great gift of hope---the virtue which enables us to meet all our tomorrows courageously and cheerfully. Hope's whole secret is that it trusts absolutely in the Lord's goodness and providence. St. Pope Pius X coined a golden formula in this regard. "The future," he says, "is in God's hands, and therefore in very good hands."

Christ and the New Millennium

What the year 2000 and the new-born millennium highlight most dramatically is the mystery of Jesus and his meaning for mankind. So profound was the impact he made on human history that, in Fulton Sheen's phrase, "he split it in two." That is, we actually number our years as coming before and after his birth. It was this factor which prompted Pope John Paul II to declare 2000 a Jubilee Year in celebration of the Christ-Child's 2000th birthday and the dawn of Christianity's third millennium.

Now because we Christians believe that the Christ-Child was really and truly God in human form, the Son of God sent to redeem sinful humanity and lead it to eternal life, the millennial Jubilee is, above all, an occasion for rejoicing in the gift of salvation. Pope John Paul II emphasized this point, further exhorting us to make 2000 an occasion for deepening our spiritual lives and kindling our zeal for God's kingdom.

Eternal and Emmanuel

"In these fleeting days of ours, Christ lived only a brief span; but he is the Eternal Day born of Eternal Day." Thus did St. Augustine attest his faith in the true humanity and divinity of the God-Man. Because both divine and human nature coexist in Christ, he consequently had a dual birth. On the one hand, he is the Son of God---the Second Person of the Trinity eternally begotten in the Father's mind as the full expression of his infinite perfections. St. John accordingly refers to him as the Father's Word.

On the other hand, this Divine Person is equally the time-born Son of the Virgin Mary. That is to say, he also had a human birth; this took place at the first real-life Christmas, nine months after his conception in Mary's womb. Thus the Word was made flesh and began his human existence, entering the stage of this world as the Babe of Bethlehem. "A speechless child," to quote St. Augustine's play on words, "is the Word of God."

What all this amounts to saying is that the mystery of Jesus is really the mystery of the Incarnation. The Eternal became Emmanuel---God in human form, God like us, with us, for us. St. Paul's formula sums it up neatly: "In Christ the whole plenitude of deity is embodied, and dwells in him" (Col 2:9). The Incarnation is therefore with good reason hailed by Newman as "the most stupendous event which can ever take place on earth." And he goes on to say: "After it and hereafter, I do not see how we can scruple at any miracle on the mere ground of its being unlikely to happen."

Eternity Into Time

That sacred and unique moment when the Word became flesh in the Virgin's womb has been described as "the point of intersection of the timeless with time." For it was then that the eternally-begotten Son of God entered our time-world as the Son of a human mother, so becoming a member of the human race and caught up inextricably into its history.

Therefore we duly speak of him as "the Jesus of history---an historical figure approaching us in time." Which truth takes on profound new depths when we recall that the Son of God, albeit during his mortal days a pilgrim through time like ourselves, transcends time inasmuch as he has an eternal existence. More than that, he is time's Creator and Lord. "It was through him," Scripture affirms, "that God created this world of time" (Heb 1:2)

Why, then, let us be quite clear, did the God-Man take on a human existence in our time-world? He did so in order to lead our time-bound selves into his own eternal life. As the risen Saviour he now dwells in the glorious heavenly world without end. But, faithful to his promise, he nonetheless continues to abide with us sacramentally here on earth, and will do so till the end of the world (cf. Mt 28: 20). Thus does the Jesus of history become the Jesus of faith, the contemporary of every successive generation. As a Polish hymn proclaims, "Christ walks with mankind through the centuries."

We Share God's Life

But how, it may be asked, does the Jesus of faith bring his sanctifying self and action into our world down the ages? The answer is: through his Church, which is his mystical body. By means of its multiform agency he brings us a share in his own divine life, which we rightly term "supernatural." The theological codeword for this life is "grace." And because grace is literally a participation in the life of the Trinity, its possession, St. Thomas assures us, means that our time-enclosed lives are already here and now caught up into God's eternity.

The life of grace is channelled to us chiefly through the sacraments, pre-eminently Christ's masterpiece sacrament---the Eucharist. Thanks to it and through it, not only is the Saviour's true presence produced under the sacramental species of bread and wine but his Good Friday sacrifice is reproduced in the Eucharistic ritual. Thus does time's Author and Lord reactivate and re-present in our midst and for our sanctification his great act of redeeming love performed on the altar of the cross nearly two millennia ago. Thus too does the risen Jesus lovingly and lavishly enrich our lives here below with the treasures of the world to come. This realization inspired Dante to write: "To know Christ is to know how to make our lives eternal."

Time Enters Eternity

As things so happened, it was a census held in the Roman Empire which created the circumstances leading to Bethlehem's becoming Our Lord's birthplace. St. Luke records that a decree had gone out from the emperor Augustus enjoining that his worldwide subjects, including those in the province of Palestine, should be registered. Accordingly St. Joseph and Mary headed for their ancestral centre---Bethlehem. And there it was that they, and the new-born Saviour, duly came to be officially inscribed among the citizens of this world.

A number of spiritual writers have pointed out the deeper

significance of this. Christ became an earthly citizen so that we might one day be enlisted in the citizenry of Heaven. He was enrolled as a subject of an earthly ruler so that we might become subjects forever of the eternal King. He became an inhabitant of the City of Man in order that we might dwell happily and everlastingly in the City of God.

In a well-known text Christ is referred to as "Alpha and Omega...the one who was, who is, and who is to come" (Apoc 1:8). This tells us that he is not only the origin of our existence but its final goal, and that he, and he alone, gives time its true direction and authentic meaning. The text further implies that we are pilgrims on our way through this world of clocks and calendars to the sanctuary of eternal life where Christ is enthroned in glory. Yet this same Christ, St. Ignatius reassures us, is ever at our side here on earth as "the companion and support of our pilgrimage."

Pope John Paul II frequently dwells on this theme. "With Christ," he writes, "eternity has entered human life. Now human life is called to make the journey with him through time to eternity. And we go in the same direction he has taken: towards the Father."

Biography In Advance

There is another, and altogether amazing, indication of the Word Incarnate's transcendence over time. It lies in the fact that numerous key details relating to his life and career as the Messiah were prophesied well in advance. This gives him the unique distinction, as Chesterton noted, of being the only man born into this world whose biography was written beforehand.

The life of Jesus began to take recorded shape a thousand years and more before his birth. That is to say, a long succession of Old Testament prophets contributed variously to the slowly-emerging composite picture of the promised Messiah. Their individual predictions and foretellings come together in the inspired writings, piece by piece, to form what might be called the messianic mosaic. With pinpoint accuracy it portrays the long-awaited Promised One, the Christ of the gospels, the Jesus of history. Incidentally, this advance messianic picture likewise constitutes a further corroboration of Christ's divine status.

The Main Prophecies

As was stated earlier, a prophetic build-up of the promised Saviour's life and lifework stretched back well over a thousand years. Let us now consider a selection of the more salient of these foreshadowings and prefigurations relative to the Messianic Lord. To begin with, he would have a forerunner---John the Baptist, who in fact was himself prophesied. The future Messiah would belong to David's lineage and be born in Bethlehem of a virgin mother. Wise men would come to adore him; there would be a massacre of infants on his account; and his parents would take him to safety in Egypt, returning in due course to Nazareth, where he would grow up and work as an artisan.

Subsequently the Messiah would become a preacher, wonder-worker and healer of the sick. He would possess superabundant spiritual power and establish his kingdom of truth and holiness. He would make a triumphal entry into Jerusalem mounted on an ass. He would cleanse the temple of traffickers. He would be betrayed by an intimate associate. His enemies would bring false accusations against him and hand him over to the Gentiles for trial. He would be mocked, buffeted, spat upon, scourged. Meanwhile his close followers would desert him. He would be crucified along with malefactors. He would be offered gall and vinegar. His death would be attended by convulsions of nature. His side would be pierced by a lance, but not a bone of his body would be broken. Lots would be cast for his vesture. He would be buried in a rich man's grave. He would rise from the tomb. Later he would ascend into Heaven. He would be a priest like Melchisedech, and a daily offering of sacrifice to God would be made far and wide. His kingdom and dominion would be universal and everlasting.

This prophetic preview of Christ's life unmistakably points towards his divine status. Even more cogently do the sensational miracles he performed during his public life, including the raising of the dead to life. But the definitive and clinching proof of Christ's divinity was the miracle that out-miracled all others, namely, his auto-resurrection from the grave. This it was that finally convinced his disillusioned followers, whose faith had been shattered by his passion and death, that he was truly the Son of God.

The Appeal of Christ

We noted earlier that such was the impact Christ made on human history that, in Fulton Sheen's words, "he split it in two." Accordingly a Jubilee Year was decreed by the Holy Father in celebration of his 2000th birthday and 20 centuries of Christianity.

But Christ has made an equally mighty impact during that time on the lives of untold multitudes in each succeeding generation. Men, women and children from every country and continent have come to believe in him and seek to model their lives on his own. Nor for them was the gospel Jesus merely a beloved and inspiring figure from the past, a distant Someone at whom they must needs gaze back wistfully across a centuries-wide gulf.

On the contrary, the Word Incarnate they worshipped was the Jesus of faith, a living, loving presence in their everyday lives. He was their model of holiness, the forgiver of sins, the source of peace and happiness, the comforter in times of trial and suffering, the teacher who is the Way, the Truth and the Life, the God-Man whose heavenly home awaits those who remain faithful to him until death.

The countless millions of the Saviour's followers in different lands and epochs would all agree with every word of Dostoyevsky's testimony: "I believe there is nothing more beautiful, more profound, more appealing, more virile or more perfect than Christ." They would likewise agree with St. Bernard's personal tribute to the Saviour: "I have found the heart of a king, the heart of a brother, the heart of a friend."

Jesus, Strength of Martyrs

It has been said of those who bear witness to Christ by their faith and faithfulness that they translate the gospel score into the music of their everyday lives. We call them his confessors, many of whom have achieved heroic virtue. But some of his confessors have been called to witness in a still more heroic way to Christ and his teaching. These are his martyrs, put to death on account of him and his cause, and their blood has been poured out in every century in countries far and wide.

The story of the martyrs is epic and inspiring. It starts off with the apostles, all of whom, except St. John, sealed their faith with their blood. The subsequent three centuries of Christianity saw the martyrdom of tens of thousands of Christ's disciples at the hands of the pagan Roman Empire, which was determined to crush and exterminate the new-born faith centred upon Jesus of Nazareth. But as martyrdoms multiplied, so did the number of fresh believers. Hence arose the adage: "The blood of the martyrs is the seed of the Church."

This pattern of persecution has been repeated time and again throughout Christian history in lands right across the globe. Here honourable mention can be made of the galaxy of martyrs who suffered during persecution times in England, Scotland, Wales and Ireland. Likewise we call to mind the thrilling story of those outstanding heroes who shed their blood on the North American continent.

Even to read about these courageous men, women and children makes us thrill with pride and admiration. For they remained steadfastly faithful to Christ and his teaching in the face of unutterable agony, torture and torment. Besides inspiring us and firing our faith and ardour by their heroism, the glorious company of martyrs now intercede for us from their place in Heaven. And the special grace they surely stand to gain for us as we head into the new millennium is that of constancy and generosity in living our faith.

Christianity's Benefits to the World

It is widely recognized that Christ's life and teaching have richly benefited the course of civilization and culture ever since the gospel was first preached by the Apostles. Volumes have been written on Christianity's profound effects in a wide range of fields. Art, architecture, music, sculpture, literature, theatre --- these owe much to the inspiration flowing from Christian values.

Enormous too are the beneficial effects of Christianity on human standards and the quality of human life. The dignity and worth of the human person and his inalienable rights; respect for womankind and their basic equality with men; the care of the poor, the sick, the aged, the homeless, the marginalised---these and other deserving areas of human life have received a mighty impetus from the gospel of love, justice and compassion preached by Christ.

Add to this the inestimable benefits deriving from the role, the pivotal role, Christianity has played in the fields of education, science and learning. Certainly the past two millennia bear abundant witness to the floodtide of social, cultural and humanitarian blessings flowing to humanity from the life and teaching of Jesus of Nazareth.

A New Springtime

Nobody is more optimistic and buoyant about the new millennium's spiritual prospects than Pope John Paul II. Its opening Jubilee Year, he confidently predicts, is due to usher in "a new springtime of Christian life...a new civilization founded on the one, holy and merciful God, and fostering a humanity reconciled in love."

This encouraging outlook reflects the Holy Father's own

glowing faith and unbounded confidence in the Lord of history, whose 2000th birthday has been proclaimed by him "a year of favour from the Lord" (Lk 4:19). And the significance of this Jubilee Year is that it marks a momentous and providential milestone in salvation history as mankind marches ahead into the third millennium.

The Pope goes on to explain that human history has just entered a very historic and significant *chairos*, that is, a propitious era superabundantly blessed with divine grace, an era in which God's creative and redeeming love will reach out prodigally to us with fresh initiatives and unparalleled generosity. So for all mankind this is a time for spiritual greatness. "Together we are called," the Holy Father exhorts us, "to build the future, basing it on the love of God and neighbour, and so establish a civilization of love."

Clearly, then, the Holy Father's message is likewise a call to holiness. Christianity's new springtime, he urges, requires that we develop a deep sorrow for sin and become giants in faith, hope and charity. But besides being a time for holiness, it is equally a time for evangelization and zeal for souls. God wills that every person without exception should come to know the truth and reach eternal salvation (cf. I Tim 2: 4).

Hunger for the Gospel

In subsequent chapters we shall see how Christ's gospel message serves as a blueprint for the brave new world of the third millennium and the longed-for civilization of love.

Little though many of them realize it, untold multitudes of our contemporaries are hungering for this gospel. The reason is that it answers all the big questions hanging over human lives---questions such as the mystery of God, the point and purpose of our existence, the evil of sin, the riddle of human suffering and mortality, the realities that lie beyond time and space.

Above all, the gospel brings us the good news of God's tremendous love for each single one of us. Everyone can look at a crucifix and make the same tremendous claim as did St. Paul: "He loved me and delivered himself for me" (Gal 2: 20). Someone who specially cherished this text was St. Louis, the king of France; he was constantly thrilled at the very thought that Jesus had not only died expressly for him and his eternal redemption but was now an ever-present Companion and Friend along the road of life.

The power and appeal of the gospel message were well expressed by Leo Tolstoy. On embracing the Christian faith he wrote: "I have discovered in Christ's gospel a new world. Nor had I ever imagined it had such depths to it." His former sense of futility and despair, he went on to say, had been replaced by "a new joy in life, a joy that will be uninterrupted by death."

Blueprint for God 2000

The gospel's underlying secret, of course, is that it is the prime source of the God-Man's revelation and the fountainhead of his teaching. Newman referred to these four brief accounts of Christ's life and doctrine as "our principal treasures." For in them we discover the key themes of Christian theology---everything from the mystery of the Trinity and the God of creation and redemption to the foundation of the Church and the reality of the four last things (death, judgment, Heaven and Hell). In addition, we find in the gospels a clear guide to moral goodness, the essence of which is the imitation of Christ.

As was to be expected, prayer features prominently in the gospel, its summit and crown being the Lord's prayer, so-called because it was taught us by Christ himself. Such is its genius that its component parts cover the core themes of Christ's message. Tertullian saw this very clearly. "The Lord's Prayer," he told his readers, "presents a synthesis of the whole gospel."

For this reason, as the following chapters set out to show, the sevenfold petitions of Christ's masterpiece prayer offer an ideal practical framework for our study of God 2000 - the loving triune Lord whom we ask, and confidently expect, to bless our third millennium with a fresh Christian springtime and a civilization of gospel love.

Chapter TWO

GOD OUR LOVING FATHER

"How beautiful it is to have a Father in Heaven." This was an exhortation frequently on the lips of St. John Vianney. Like many a saint before and after, he was ardently devoted to the Our Father prayer, which Christians have always treasured as a most precious gift from the God-Man himself. Its whole appeal and power is that it expresses, in simple language and in a wonderfully compact way, all the basic duties and needs that bind us humans to our Father-Creator in Heaven. Indeed, the prayer provides the essential building materials for the civilization of love waiting to be constructed by mankind with the help of God's grace during the third millennium.

Nor is it only saints and theologians that have sung the Our Father's praises down the ages. A great diversity of people have done so as well. Take, for example, the two military geniuses who clashed famously at Waterloo---the Duke of Wellington and Napoleon. "The Lord's Prayer," said the former, "contains the sum-total of religion and morals." As for Napoleon, his tribute was: "Do you wish to find out the really sublime? Recite the Lord's Prayer."

Why We Call God Our Father

In the first place, the Lord of Heaven and earth created us human beings---and did so in a wonderfully privileged way, namely, as bearing in ourselves his very own image and likeness. Secondly, the Creator's fatherly love never fails to govern us, as he does all creation, through his providence; but again he does so in our regard in a privileged way. For, as St. Thomas explains, the Father's government of his sub-human creation is as "slaves of his will," whereas he faithfully respects our human status as "masters of ourselves" by never coercing our freedom. As for the third reason why we address God as Father, it is that, in and through his own beloved Son, he has adopted us, giving us "the spirit of adoption as sons, whereby we cry Abba, Father" (Rom 8: 15).

What Do We Owe God Our Father?

To begin with, we owe him honour and praise, not only on our lips but in our hearts (cf. Is 29: 13). And, too, we must honour him with our entire body-soul selves (cf. 1 Cor 6:20).

Next, we owe it to God that we imitate him by striving after perfection. Our Lord made this duty perfectly clear when he enjoined: "Be ye perfect as also your heavenly Father is perfect" (Mt 5: 48). Our imitation of God must also extend to loving him with our whole heart, soul and strength. St. Paul says explicitly: "Be ye imitators of God as most dear children and walk in love" (Eph 5: 1,2). Thirdly we are to imitate God by showing mercy to others.

Besides honouring and imitating God, we owe him total obedience because of his dominion over us and also because his Son became obedient to him unto death (cf. Phil 2:8). Finally, we owe it to God that we love our neighbour as ourselves and show him reverence and respect, since he is our brother and one of God's beloved children. St. John emphasized this point." He who does not love his brother whom he sees," he reasons, "how can he love God whom he does not see?" (I Jn 4: 20). Indeed, St. Thomas points out that in the Lord's Prayer we pray not just for ourselves but for all in general precisely in order to show and exercise our neighbourly love.

The Prayer of Intimacy

So by addressing God as Father, we affirm first of all that he is the almighty Creator, the ultimate origin of everyone and everything in the universe. At the same time the title tells us that the Lord of

Heaven and earth looks on all human beings with deep parental love and concern. The Aramaic word for Father---Abba, uttered by Jesus and employed by the early Christians (Mt 14: 36; Rom 8:15)---expresses warm and familiar affection with nuances of intimacy and tenderness.

"God's first gift to me," each of us can say with St. Bernard, was myself." This is a profound truth and a most consoling one. It means that my own personal being, my own unique selfhood, is the Father's special creation and the object of his personal love and care. Hence each of us beloved children of our Father-God can address him as did the Psalmist: "Author, thou, of my inmost being, didst thou not form me in my mother's womb? I praise thee for my wondrous fashioning, for all the wonders of thy creation. Of my soul thou hast full knowledge" (Ps 138: 13-15).

So there is nothing remote or abstract about the God of the Lord's Prayer. Still less is he to be regarded as the terrible Jehovah, the awesome Elohim and Lord of hosts. Rather, in Browning's words, "the All-Great is the All-Loving too." So loving indeed is he, Padre Pio used to say, that "he loves us beyond understanding."

The God of Planet Earth

God 2000 is, then, our all-loving, all-caring Father in heaven, and by his providence the world-wide human family has just entered its third Christian millennium. According to a recent United Nations statistic, this family now totals six billion, a stupendous multitude of "beings breathing thoughtful breath, travellers between life and death."

Though the human family comprises such a gigantic total, yet each and every member without exception is cherished with paternal love by the God of Heaven and earth. St. Augustine's prayer well expresses this wonderful and exciting reality: "All-powerful God, you care for each one of us as if you loved him alone, yet you care for all as if all were but one."

The habitat God has provided for humankind on its pilgrimage through time is this good earth of ours. Being a planet, it is ever moving through space at tremendous speed as it cruises along the rim of the Milky Way. Which means to say that our planetary home is equivalently a spacecraft of a kind, while we six billion passengers on board are space-travellers on a perpetual orbit around the sun. As for our speed, it is something like 18 miles per *second*. And, as if this were not enough, the earth is at the same time spinning on its axis at approximately 1000 miles per hour. This accounts for the fact that we experience successive days and nights as our hemisphere alternately faces towards or away from the sun.

Mention of days and nights recalls what we already know full well: we are also time-travellers. That is to say, starting with the day we were born, we are embarked on a non-stop journey through the days, the months and the years. For ours is essentially a time-world, a world of sunrises and sunsets, birthdays and anniversaries, a world closely regulated by clocks and calendars. Moreover, the very units we use to measure time are precisely those that relate to the earth's movements in space. For these give rise not only to days and nights but also to years---365 days being the time it takes the earth to do a complete orbit around the sun.

God's Existence

In saying all this we are dealing with the handiwork of our Creator and loving Father in Heaven. For he it was who made and maintains this immense, mysterious universe. St. Theresa of Lisieux never got over the wonder and awe she experienced on first seeing the ocean; it brought home to her with stunning effect the infinite power and majesty of our heavenly Father. Similarly St. Ignatius would spend hours communing with the Divine Majesty as he contemplated the night sky---that distant and beautiful fairyland of stars beyond all numbering, each of them moving through space on its appointed orbit at a dizzying speed. This was the same spectacle that inspired G.M. Hopkins to write: "I kiss my hand to the stars, lovely-asunder starlight, wafting him out of it."

The Psalmist too felt strongly drawn towards the Infinite Being who fashioned the glittering star-worlds: "I look up at those heavens of thine, the work of thy hands, at the moon and the stars, which thou hast set in their places...O Lord, our Master, how the majesty of thy name fills all the earth" (Ps 8: 4,10).

As something of the artist is always revealed in his work, so too is the Father-Creator mirrored in his creation. Thus the immensity of space reflects his infinity and majesty, while the order and mathematical precision so patently operative in the world of stars reflect his intelligence and consummate planning. Again the Psalmist has words for this experience. "See how the skies," he says, "proclaim God's glory, how the vault of Heaven betrays his craftmanship" (Ps 18: 2).

The Master Craftsman

Now craftsmanship implies design, arrangement, order. And these qualities are abundantly evident not only in the night sky but throughout creation. For this reason the Greeks called the universe a cosmos---a system exactly planned and coordinated down to the tiniest detail. To assert that it is the product of mere chance has rightly been described as suicide of the mind. "I would be prostituting my intelligence," Thomas Edison declared, "if I denied the existence of a Supreme Power."

It is worth noting, however, that some who deny God's existence are in fact rejecting a mistaken notion of the deity, so mistaken in some cases that it amounts to a caricature. For example, the vague and superficial notion that God is a grandfatherly old man with a white beard is rightly rejected as being primitive and unworthy. But, once people come to form a correct idea of God, their opposition tends to weaken and die, since "we needs must love the highest when we see it."

It is not unknown, in fact, for former atheists to conceive a tremendous, even passionate, love of God. A notable example was Blessed Charles de Foucauld, who subsequently said about his conversion experience: "The moment I realised that God existed, I knew I could not do otherwise than live for him alone."

The God of Beauty

God has many attributes or perfections, all of them to an infinite degree. Thus he is immense, powerful, wise, good, holy, just, beautiful. And, as was said earlier, all these qualities are mirrored a millionfold in the created world, each instance pointing unerringly to God as to its all-perfect fountainhead. But the attribute that seems to exercise a particularly strong attraction over many souls is the divine beauty. Certainly this was the case with St. Augustine. "O God our Father supremely good," he wrote, "you are the beauty of all things beautiful."

A notable modern example was the former black slave, Giuseppina Bakhita, who hailed from the Sudan and was brought to Italy in 1910 by her owner and master. She has given rare expression to the human quest for the all-beautiful Author of the beauty so manifest throughout creation. In her own words: "Seeing the sun, the moon and the stars, I said to myself: 'Who could be the Master of these beautiful things?' And I felt a great desire to see him, to know him, and to pay him homage."

On obtaining her freedom, she became a Canossian Daughter of Charity. So profound was the effect on her of discovering the God of beauty that she subsequently consecrated herself to living entirely for him in the holy beauty of religious life. She died in 1947 and has since been canonized.

The Divine Family

When the Eternal Word came on earth to reveal truths about God and human destiny, it was to be expected that his revelation would include a surprise or two. It certainly did. And the loveliest surprise of all was that God is not a solitary but a threesome, that is, a trio of persons, a trinity, a three-member family---Father, Son and Holy Spirit. So when we adore the Supreme Being it is three distinct

Selves that gaze out at us. These three Selves are co-eternal and co-equal, inasmuch as each possesses the identical divine substance, the selfsame being. In other words, each Person is in God; yet each is fully and completely the one and undivided Godhead.

It is the Father who has as it were prime possession of the divine life. For he is the source, the unoriginated origin, of the deity. He begets his Son in a beginningless process as the living reflection and expression of his own perfections. This Son is the Second Person of the Trinity and is known as the Father's Word.

Sharing in Their Life

Between Father and Son, the Begetter and the Only-Begotten, a reciprocal love is exchanged from endless ages. Expressing as it does the infinitely perfect attraction between two divine Persons, their love too is necessarily infinite in its perfection. Whence it further follows that it has the perfection of being a divine Person, alive with the common life of its joint Producers. This Third Person, who literally personifies the mutual love uniting Father and Son and constitutes the living bond between them, accordingly possesses the selfsame being and is co-equal with them in all respects. We know this Love-Person as the Holy Spirit, the Third Person of the Trinity.

The whole Christian life, then, is essentially a sharing in the communion between the three Divine Persons. And we can commune at will with any single one of the Three without in any way separating the Godhead. Thus when we glorify the Father we do so through the Son and in the Holy Spirit.

What also follows is that everything Our Lord communicates to us is the fruit of his intimate union with the Father. As he attests in the gospel, "The Father and I are one...All that the Father has is mine" (Jn 10:30; 16:15). This indicates that there is complete reciprocity between Father and Son in what they know of each other, in what they are, in what they do, and in what they possess (cf. Jn 10:15; 14:10; 10;38; 17:10).

The Million Masks of God

The underlying worth and dignity of every human being is that he is by creation an image of God. In other words, his spirit is capable of remembering, of reasoning, and of making free choices. These three so-called powers or faculties of the human soul, as theologians point out, reflect respectively the three Persons of the Trinity: memory for the Father, understanding for the Son, and freedom of choice for the Holy Spirit.

"Being in the image of God," the Catholic Catechism teaches, "the human individual possesses the dignity of being a person, who is not just something but someone. He is capable of self-knowledge, of self-possession, and of freely giving himself and entering into communion with other persons." What is more, let us note, a human being is capable of knowing, loving and serving God and has been called to an eternal communion of life with him.

It is truly remarkable that, just as no two sets of fingerprints are identical, so it is with human persons. Each in his own distinctive and unrepeatable way is an image of the Holy Trinity. For this reason it has been said that man's Creator never makes imitations but only originals. In other words, each individual in his own unique way images forth the trinitarian nature of the Godhead. G.K. Chesterton was fascinated by this mystery, recognizing it as the underlying reason for the human person's immense dignity and value. It explains, he says, why in any crowded street we can observe "the million masks of God."

The Aboriginal Calamity

Nowhere did our Father in Heaven display his infinite compassion and mercy more than at the dawn of mankind's history. For he gratuitously restored our human dignity and destiny alike when these had been lost through the sin of our First Parents.

Not only were they created in God's image but had also been given a share in his divine life---that is, grace---thus elevating them to be his human likenesses. Then occurred what Newman refers to as "that terrible aboriginal calamity." Adam and Eve, standing as proxy for their innumerable progeny, transgressed the divine commandment, committing thereby what is known as Original Sin, the guilt of which was personal for them and hereditary for us.

As for their sin's penal consequences, these too were hereditary. The most serious was that, with the withdrawal of supernatural life, Adam and Eve lost their status as God's likenesses. And this loss made total shipwreck of mankind's eternal destiny. For the Father had meant our primogenitors to live in close union with him through grace in this world so as to share his glory in the everlasting world to come.

But that prospect now lay in ruins. By breaking their covenant with the Creator, Adam and Eve incurred for themselves and their descendants the inevitable consequences, the worst of which, as we have seen, was the loss of grace and the eternal beatitude to which it gave access. Among the penal results of Adam's rebellion against the Creator was the dimming of the divine image in him and the consequent weakening of his spiritual powers. Also he was now subject to ignorance, suffering, and death, as well as being inclined to sinfulness through having lost the perfect harmony between reason and natural instincts.

God to the Rescue

But the Father of mankind had compassion on his fallen human creatures, announcing to our First Parents the coming victory over evil besides their restoration from the Fall. The biblical passage in question (Gen 3:9, 15) has with good reason been called the protoevangelium, namely, the "first gospel." For it prophesies the coming of a Messiah-Redeemer, the ensuing spiritual warfare between the devil and the Woman, and her offspring's final and definitive victory over him.

What can be read into the protoevangelium is an

announcement of the New Adam---he whose sacrificial death in obedience to the Father would make superabundant amends for Adam's disobedience (cf. I Cor 15: 21,22). What can likewise be read into the text is an announcement of the New Eve---Mary, the Redeemer's sinless mother.

In a word, what the Father of mercies promised our fallen protoparents was the stupendous mystery of the Incarnation. God so loved the world that he would give his only-begotten Son as the price of human redemption and as our way to the Father. "In his measureless love," St. Irenaeus declared, "God became what we are in order that we might become what he is."

Religion has been described as "man's adventure into God." Anyway, it was to receive a mighty impetus from the Incarnation, which in turn can fairly be described as God's adventure into man. Through this adventure, a poet has said, the vast Creator became "a native of the very world he made."

The main effect of God's adventure into our world and its history is that we can once again become his likenesses through the grace flowing from Christ through his Church. It is divine grace that restores us to the Father's friendship, making us his adopted children, brothers and sisters of the God-Man. Through and with this God-Man we can now address the First Person of the Trinity as "Abba, Father." And through and with the God-Man we are destined to spend eternal life in the Father's heavenly home.

Return of the Prodigals

One of Our Lord's most powerful and eloquent parables was that of the prodigal son (cf. Lk 15: 32). It applies equally to the individual penitent sinner and collectively to sinful humanity at large.

Our heavenly Father is featured most prominently in the parable. His wayward child has wandered far from home and is in a desperate plight, finally ending up in that most demeaning of livelihoods for a Jew---feeding swine. It is awareness of his miserable state that prompts the prodigal to "come to his senses." He decides to return to the peace and plenty of his Father's house. And in the event the welcome he receives is overwhelmingly warm. His delighted Father goes to meet him half-way and issues instructions for a celebratory feast. Meanwhile he puts a ring on his repentant son's finger as a symbol of his covenanted love, wraps him in a robe symbolical of a new life, and supplies him with shoes as a sign of his regained dignity.

Alternatively we can identify the prodigal son with the human race after the primordial tragedy of original sin. It was sunk in guilt and wretchedness. But forgiveness and mercy were extended to it by "the God and Father of Our Lord Jesus Christ, a gentle Father and the God of all consolation" (2 Cor 1:3). Once again his heavenly home became the summit and goal for all who remain faithful to his commandments.

Our Homeward Journey

Very significantly the Hebrew word for "Father's house" also means "family." Our Father-Creator's present-day human family---all six billion of us---needs to come ever-closer to him during this new millennium through repentance and prayer, so preparing itself for the feast of eternal life in his heavenly household. All members without exception of this global family are, through sins of commission and omission, prodigal sons and daughters making their pilgrim way day after day through this world to our eternal homeland. The Father has given us his Son to bring us back to him, and his Holy Spirit to sanctify, guide us and lead us on that lifelong journey.

Additional helps provided by our all-solicitous Father-God include a guardian angel for each of us prodigals on the long pilgrimage of life. And in a special way we have to thank the God of Providence for giving us Mary as our mother. Lovingly and zealously the sinless daughter of the Father urges and assists all his children and hers to return safely to that heavenly homeland where she is queen and mistress for ever.

God 2000

Chapter THREE

THE GOD OF HOLINESS

Each time we say "hallowed be thy name" in the Lord's Prayer, we are reaching right down to the grass roots of our being. For as God's rational creatures it is our bounden duty, besides crowning privilege, to hallow "the Father of all mankind, who is Lord of all, works in us all, and is in us all" (Eph 4: 6). Moreover, in saying "hallowed be thy name" we venture at the same time into the innermost mystery of the Divine Being, our Almighty Maker, he who is the Wholly Other, the Infinitely Holy.

So central to the Our Father is "hallowed be thy name" that it implicitly embodies all the other petitions. The reason is that it engages us at the deepest level of our being, fashioned and called as we are by God to be holy like himself. And when in our lives we fulfill that calling as we should, we are at the same time contributing valuable building blocks towards the civilization of love waiting to be erected through the grace of God 2000 and our collaborative efforts.

Explaining this Petition

We need first of all to look into the meaning of "hallow." It is an archaic word coming from the Old English "halig," meaning holy. So in the Our Father we are literally asking that God's name be made holy. As a noun, "hallow" stands for a holy person (hence the feast of All Hallows, meaning All Saints). Our all-holy God is therefore the Infinite Hallow.

We find a clear explanation of what "hallowed be thy

name" means in St. Cyprian's treatise on the Lord's Prayer. "It is not that we intend in this petition," he says, "to make God holy by our prayers. Rather, we are asking him that his name be made holy in us. For how could God be made holy, he who is the source of all holiness?" The saint's concluding comment is also worth noting: "We pray every day for God's name to be hallowed because of the need we have for daily sanctification."

In biblical language, hallowing God's name means virtually the same as giving him praise on account of his glory, that is, his self-knowledge and self-love. Now these, being divine perfections, are infinite. Wherefore God's internal glory is infinite and thus incapable of receiving any increase.

But the same does not apply to God's so-called external glory, namely, what we and the rest of creation owe him by way of praise and honour. Because it comes from creatures, this glory is finite; consequently God's external glory can be increased and magnified. Indeed, it imperatively demands to be increased and magnified at all times and in all places, since creation's whole purpose is to render the maximum possible glory to its Author.

What Visible Creation Owes God

A further preliminary point requiring clarification is the meaning of "name" as found in the Our Father. It is a biblical expression signifying a person's reputation and due rights. What, then, we must now ask, are our heavenly Father's due rights with regard to ourselves and this world of ours?

Basically they are twofold. First is that our Father-God is to be accepted and duly esteemed by mankind as its all-holy Lord, and that every human being without exception should keep his commandments and live a holy life. Secondly, we who are equivalently the messiahs and princes of nature through being endowed with God's noble gift of reason are meant to glorify him in our use and enjoyment of visible creation, being careful to avoid abusing it through sin. In addition, the Father expects that we render him due thanks and praise for the multiple blessings he bestows on us through the created world.

The Call to Holiness

So our first and principal task in meeting the Father's just demands is our personal sanctification. We are reminded of this duty on practically every page of Scripture. St. Paul, for example, states that "the God and Father of Our Lord Jesus Christ chose us that we should be holy and blameless before him in love" (Eph 1: 34). And Our Lord himself has enjoined us to be perfect even as our heavenly Father is perfect (cf. Mt 5: 48).

This scriptural call to holiness carries a special resonance during the Jubilee Year 2000, which the Roman Pontiff has designated as a time for conversion and personal renewal. In proclaiming the call he is at the same time echoing the message of Vatican II. "All Christ's faithful," it urges, "no matter what their rank or station, have a vocation to the fullness of Christian life and the perfection of charity. All have an invitation, which is binding, to the pursuit of holiness and perfection in their own station of life."

Accordingly the Holy Father has appealed for us to kindle within ourselves "a new ardour and true longing for holiness," so that our faith may be strengthened and our witness become more authentic. At the same time he urges us to develop a keener sensitivity towards the poor and needy.

Jesus, Source of Life and Holiness

Clearly, then, our pursuit of personal holiness is the prime and principal way by which we are to hallow the name of our Father in Heaven. And if it be asked what constitutes personal holiness, the short answer is that it is nothing other than the imitation of Christ. For he is our Master and Model, the Holy One of Israel whom we are to follow as our Way, Truth and Life (cf. Jn 14: 6).

St. Paul saw personal holiness primarily in terms of Christ

living within us and sharing intimately in our lives (cf. Gal 2:20). This profound mystery of the Saviour's indwelling presence and activity was referred to by Tennyson as "his being working in my own, the footsteps of his life in mine."

Help from the Saints

A further help towards hallowing our Father's name through holiness of life is to familiarise ourselves with the lives of his saints, whose example serves both to inspire us and spur us on. Despite their profoundly diverse human qualities and social backgrounds, the saints display one common factor, one instantly recognizable identification mark. It is this: they loved God with their entire heart, mind, soul and strength, and, for his sake, their neighbours as well (cf. Mt 22: 37-39). Through this love, and by modelling themselves, as Our Lord prescribed, on the Father's own perfections, they hallowed him by making heroic sanctity their goal.

In carrying out this programme, the saints were implementing the exhortation of St. Gregory of Nyssa: "We must contemplate the beauty of the Father without ceasing, and adorn our own souls accordingly." The whole secret of the saints is that they gave themselves entirely to this programme, becoming in consequence resplendent with moral beauty. They each display in their distinctive ways what Pascal calls "the serene, silent beauty of a holy life." Nor has any saint attained this spiritual beauty to the same degree as the Word Incarnate's sinless mother. Rightly she is called the Panhagia, the all-holy one. And, as the lives of the saints further testify, Marylikeness is the sure road to Christlikeness.

The Role of Love

The primacy of love in the hierarchy of Christian values was emphasized by the author of the Imitation of Christ. "Love knows no bounds," he says, "but burns with boundless fervour...He is truly great who has great love."

In other words, there is a living equation between love and

holiness, as God's heroic ones demonstrate so glowingly. Through loving and serving the Infinite Hallow with their entire being and doing, they duly hallow him by living Christlike lives. Indeed, each in their own individual way, the saints exemplify Charles de Foucauld's stirring exhortation to all who bear Christ's name: "Everything about us, all that we are, should proclaim the gospel from the housetops. Our whole being should be a living witness, a reflection, of Jesus."

Holiness is Kind

A celebrated theologian and preacher in the early Church, St. John Chrysostom, when speaking of our vocation to be holy and thereby glorify the Father, laid great stress on the importance of kindness. "You cannot call the God of all kindness your Father," he warns, "if you preserve a cruel and inhuman heart. For in this case you no longer have in you the marks of your heavenly Father's kindness."

The same theme recurs in many other spiritual authorities. St. John of the Cross, for example, places heavy emphasis on the value of kindness in our pursuit of holiness, since without it God is gravely displeased and dishonoured. Mother Teresa had the same message, reminding us that we are called to be "the light of God's kindness" to others. She is also on record as saying: "Be kind and merciful...Be the living expression of God's kindness---kindness in your face, kindness in your eyes, kindness in your smile, kindness in your warm greeting."

As we would expect, the selfsame lesson was taught by St. Paul. Besides characterizing Christian love as being, among other things, kind, he counsels us to "disarm malice with kindness" (I Cor 13: 4; Rom 12: 21).

The Value of Prayer

As every saint without exception would affirm, our paramount need on the road to holiness is prayer. St. Augustine compared the man who does not pray to a tree without roots. Prayer has also been likened to a lifeline or umbilical cord linking us to the living God. And the Son of this living God has taught us by his own example to make prayer the very breath of our lives; also he expressly revealed our heavenly Father's desire to be adored by us "in spirit and in truth" (Jn 4: 24). Prayer is accordingly an imperative duty as well as vital necessity. Without it our hallowing of the heavenly Father would falter and die.

It will be helpful to recall that prayer has four basic functions or modes, each serving in its specific way to hallow God. They can be summarised as follows: prayer worships and adores God; it begs his forgiveness when we sin; it asks him for benefits and favours; and it thanks him for his many gifts.

To begin with adoration and worship. Through it we pay our Author and Maker the creaturely homage we owe him. "Thou mastering me, God," we can address him in the poet's words, "giver of breath and bread, world's strand, sway of the sea, Lord of living and dead." Because he has absolute dominion over us, it is only right and fitting that we should humbly bow down before God, recognizing his total sovereignty over ourselves and all creation.

Contrition, Petition, Thanksgiving

As St. Ignatius saw so vividly, man was created by God to praise, reverence and serve him in this world and thereby merit eternal happiness in the next. And what the saint saw no less vividly is that the mighty Creator is likewise the all-holy God of the commandments, the God of conscience. Consequently, when we offend him by breaking his commandments we must without fail express our heartfelt contrition. This is the second function of prayer; it hallows the Father's name by expressing sorrow for sin and purposing amendment.

In addition to being sinful creatures repeatedly having to ask for divine forgiveness, we are in so many ways limited, dependent and needy. This accounts for prayer's third function, which is to ask God to supply our legitimate requirements. All-important among these is our daily bread; hence Our Lord, in teaching us the Our Father, made bread representative of our fundamental earthly needs.

We can be sure that our Father-God is pleased and hallowed by the faith and trust his children place in him when petitioning for benefits and blessings. And when we thank him for these---and so implement prayer's fourth function---he is no less pleased and hallowed.

How God Hallows Us

As we have been seeing, God hallows us in order that we might in turn hallow him. And to this end he provides us with a number of sanctifying agents and agencies. Chief among these agents, it goes without saying, is the Sanctifier, the Third Person of the Trinity, who unites us with the Father and the Son. Through his sevenfold gifts he helps us to stay sensitively attuned to God's holy will, docile to his every inspiration, and faithful in his service.

God's angels too play a providential and vital part as sanctifying agents in our regard. They who adore the Father unceasingly and cry "holy, holy, holy" in perpetual homage before his throne have been given charge over us to keep us in all our ways, not least the ways of worship and prayer (cf. Ps 90: 11). Through their constant care and multiple ministries our angelic friends promote our hallowing of the Father's name as they themselves do without ceasing in Heaven.

What Our Father Provides

In his loving providence the Father of mercies, the object of our hallowing, has placed at our disposal a wealth of means designed to sanctify us body and soul. We see this reality reflected in the term "Communion of Saints," which from earliest times has been a descriptive label for the Church. What it tells us is that the Church is a commonwealth of holy ones sanctified through the common wealth of holy things it has received as a legacy from the Apostles.

The currency, so to call it, of the Church's common wealth is sanctifying grace, which elevates us to the supernatural order because it is a sharing in God's own life. And this precious currency is channelled to us through certain God-given agencies by means of which he sanctifies his beloved children.

First among these agencies is the institutional Church itself; from it we receive the truths of revelation---truths that are in themselves holy and holy-making (cf. Jn 17: 19). From the Church we receive too the Sacred Scriptures, which are not only divinely inspired but inspiring, serving to instruct and sanctify us on our journey to the Father's eternal home (cf. 2 Tim 3: 16). Indeed, St. Jerome likened the sacred books to a letter from that loving Father in which he offers enlightenment and encouragement to his sons and daughters on their long homeward pilgrimage.

God's Sacramental Agencies

The next agencies to consider are the sacraments, each of which is designed to produce a specific grace for man's sanctification and closer union with the Father. First comes baptism, whereby human persons are consecrated to God and become living, flesh-and-blood temples of the indwelling Trinity. Further, this sacrament seals us with the so-called priesthood of the faithful, the essential function of which is the offering of adoration and service to the Eternal Father.

Confirmation brings an increase of the Holy Spirit's gifts, making us more docile and generous in our hallowing of the Father. And when we offend the God of the commandments through sin, the sacrament of Penance brings us his pardon and peace. As for Marriage, its grace sets up conjugal love and, too, forms human families in the likeness of the Father's divine family in Heaven. And if on our journey through this world we should incur serious illness, the sacrament of Anointing is our Father's peace-giving and tonic gift for both body and spirit. This sacrament is administered by an ordained priest, who, through the sacrament of Order, is empowered to forgive sins in God's name and, what is more, to be the minister of the Eucharist.

The Father's Best Gift

"Lord God, make us truly holy by this Eucharist, which you give us as the source of all holiness." This liturgical prayer for the feast of St. Ignatius expresses a traditional Catholic truth: namely, the Eucharist is the wellspring of holiness, the fountainhead of all grace and sànctification. St. Thomas sees the Eucharist as "the consummation of the whole spiritual life." Vatican II fully endorses this teaching. "The Eucharist," it states, "contains the whole spiritual treasure of the Church, that is, Christ himself."

The underlying mystery of the Eucharist is, of course, that it is the true presence of Christ produced by the celebrating priest's words of consecration---the words that at the same time re-present Christ's Good Friday sacrifice in ritual, sacramental form.

Nowhere is the Father more hallowed than in his Son's Eucharistic mysteries. And nowhere do we ourselves enjoy such scope for hallowing him. In the first place, our faith in the true presence of the Saviour gives praise and glory to the Father-God, whose loving initiative it was that gave us not only Emmanuel but now Emmanuel-made-Eucharist.

Secondly, as the Eucharistic liturgy makes clear, the Father features prominently within the Mass. We frequently recall his presence and invoke his name, offering him "this life-giving bread, this saving cup" and thanking him for counting us worthy to stand in his presence and serve him.

Hans Urs von Baltasar has described the Word Incarnate as "the Father's substantial Eucharist." By this he means that Christ is the perfect Thanksgiver and Hallower, eternally offering back to the Father the divine being and perfections he received from him as his Progenitor.

Communing with the Father

Holy Communion affords us a third way of uniting ourselves closely with Our Lord's Father and glorifying him. St. Elizabeth of the Trinity was granted a deep insight into this mystery; our Communions, she tells us, are in fact a participation in the Word's eternal communion with his Father. She also points out that, in receiving Holy Communion, we likewise receive, and can therefore commune with, all three Persons. Why this is so is because the three Divine Persons are inseparably united in the one Godhead, the identical and undivided Being.

This also explains why we can praise, glorify and hallow the Father when we adore the Blessed Sacrament. There we behold and worship what von Baltasar calls "the mystery of the Three Countenances...the Three-in-One mystery objectified and concretely visible in the humanity of the Word-made-Flesh."

Mother Eugenia Ravasio, a celebrated mystic in recent times, was given to understand by God the Father that the treasures of the Eucharist were expressly willed by him, so ardently desirous is he to foster through them an intimate relationship with his beloved children and move them by this means to render him due praise and glory.

Earth's Thousand Voices

A theme we frequently come across in the psalms is that all creatures are meant to glorify their almighty Creator simply by being what they are and by doing according to their God-given nature. Birds in the air and stars in the sky, fishes in the ocean and trees waving in the wind---the whole of creation comprises a cosmic temple offering praise to the Almighty.

"Earth with her thousand voices praises God." Coleridge is one of many poets that take up the same theme as the psalmist: all things without exception are meant to hallow the Lord and render him glory. Elizabeth Barret Browning, for example, exclaims in wonder, "Earth's crammed with heaven, and every common bush is afire with God." Similarly, G.M. Hopkins sees the world as "charged with the grandeur of God."

God is in created things, we learn from St. Thomas, by essence, presence and power. And consequently we recognize in creatures many reflections of God's perfections, such as his all-powerfulness, his wisdom, his beauty. Moreover, all sub-human things were created ultimately for our use and enjoyment and thus for the hallowing of the Father's name. Should we misuse or abuse created things, we are committing sin and incur the divine displeasure. Moreover, God's creation itself would, if it could, says St. Ignatius, rise up against us in protest.

By properly using things we as it were complete the Creator's work and render him praise and glory. This is what is meant when we say man is the messiah of nature. He tends it, harnesses its powers, gains from it service, produce and enjoyment, finds in it a mirror of God's majesty, and draws therefrom deep inspiration for communing with the Creator.

A notable example of this was Johann Sebastian Bach, a genius in God's world of sound and harmony. So filled was he with divine love that he dedicated each of his compositions to the Creator's glory, endeavouring to provide through his magnificent cantatas and oratorios so many echoes and glimpses of him who is the All-Beautiful and the All-Hallow.

Franciscan Rhapsodies

Another notable, indeed classic, example was St. Francis of Assisi. So totally in love was he with our Father in Heaven that he felt a creaturely kinship and communion with all his creation---the wind and the sky, the sun, the moon, the stars, mountains, flowers, trees, fire, water, the entire animal kingdom: in a word, anything and everything in this world, even the death of "our brother the body."

For him all created realities not only bespoke God's presence and goodness but demanded that through them we honour and hallow his name.

In the same Franciscan tradition was St. Maximilian Kolbe, who died as a martyr in Auschwitz in 1941. Besides loving God in and through the world of nature, he warmly welcomed modern technology and scientific progress, recognizing therein the Creator's wisdom and praising him accordingly. With reference to his apostolate of the written word, Maximilian spoke humorously of "brother motor, sister ink, and old grandmother press." He saluted and revered these and all modern inventions as man's completion of creation; what is more, they place at man's disposal valuable additional means of hallowing and serving our Father-God.

Finally, man is nature's priest in addition to being its messiah; his role is to offer it to God in praise and thanksgiving. Indeed, in the Eucharistic mysteries this offering takes on a cosmic as well as sacramental dimension. For we place on the paten, alongside the host and our own unworthy selves, that manifold of good things represented by the bread and wine. Thus the entire universe, nothing and nobody excepted, hallows the Almighty Father's name through being offered to him by our great High Priest each time he renews his redeeming sacrifice on our altars.

Chapter FOUR

THE GOD OF THE KINGDOM

"The music of the gospel leads us home." Newman's words prompt us into thinking of the gospel in terms of a symphony, a divinely composed symphony---indeed, a New World symphony of a most exalted kind. For its haunting melodies tell of God's brave new world brought into our lives by Jesus of Nazareth, a world of life, holiness and truth, a world destined to blossom into paradisal glory at the end of time.

Nor is there any doubt as to what particular theme would qualify as the leitmotif running through the gospel symphony. The expression "kingdom of God" (equivalently "kingdom of Heaven"), which was so often on Our Lord's lips, is the easy winner; it occurs nearly a hundred times altogether in the pages of the gospel. Furthermore, the expression is widely scattered across the remainder of the New Testament, while the Old Testament likewise makes frequent use of it.

So it comes as no surprise that Christ integrated the kingdom of God concept into the Our Father prayer. For it is a theme altogether central to his teaching, forming the very bottom line of his message and mission, besides constituting a key element of Christian spirituality. Accordingly he specifically taught us to ask the Father to promote his kingdom here on earth and hasten its glorious consummation in the world to come.

What God's Kingdom Means

Put in very general terms, the kingdom of God stands for everything the Father offers us in and through his Incarnate Son. Clearly this "everything" comprises a wide array of gifts, benefits and blessings, which come to us from the God of the kingdom at three distinct levels, so to call them.

First of these levels is the interior kingdom, the kingdom within that private, personal, complex world which is ourselves. "The kingdom of God is within you" (Lk 17: 21). Christ was most explicit about this reality, which clearly amounts to something both awesome and wonderful. For what it entails is that our body-soul selves become living sanctuaries or temples, playing host not only to the grace of God but to the God of grace---that is, three august Guests---indwelling us. And what brings about this marvellous effect within our selfhood is the sacrament of baptism plus the panoply of divine gifts accompanying it.

The second level at which God's kingdom touches our lives is the Church. As visible as any city situated on a hill, it is an external organisation commissioned and equipped by its Founder primarily to inaugurate the interior kingdom in human lives through baptism. The Church's further ministrations serve to nourish and promote that interior kingdom through its teaching office and sacramental apparatus. All of which ministries are geared to helping Church-members reach eternal life and so attain to the resurrection from the dead.

Mention of resurrection leads us to the third level at which the kingdom of God is designed to operate in human lives. It will be ushered in by the resurrection of the dead due to take place when Christ comes again on Judgment Day as the King of heavenly glory; which second coming was referred to by the early Christians as the Parousia. In its wake our resurrected and glorified selves will become citizens for ever in the heavenly kingdom of God, which, as long as this present world lasts, will continue to act as the shining goal and driving inspiration for the kingdom's first two stages.

We shall presently be seeing something more of these three levels, which bear out St. Cyprian's observation that God's kingdom pertains to "earthly as well as heavenly realities." Yet these levels are so vitally interconnected that in fact they represent three aspects of one and the same reality. Operating as the visible Church-kingdom, this reality initiates and services the invisible kingdom in human souls. And meanwhile this hard-pressed duo of earthly kingdoms yearn for their eventual consummation in that heavenly world where grace becomes glory and time will yield place to eternity.

The Kingdom Within Us

In practical terms, the first or interior level of God's kingdom is plainly the most significant for us pilgrims *en route* to eternal life. For it is all-decisive in determining how we stand with God at any given time, particularly at the hour of our death. Hence we owe it to ourselves that we deepen our understanding of the unseen kingdom within us, the better to cherish and safeguard it as the pearl of great price presented to us by our loving Redeemer.

When we are baptised, wrote Eckhart, the Dominican mystic, we receive no less than "God himself with all his riches." What this amounts to saying is that in my own little kingdom of self, as Shakespeare calls it, the King of Heaven and earth---all three Persons---come and make their dwelling-place. Our Lord affirmed this very explicitly: "My Father and I will come to you and make our abode with you" (Jn 14: 23).

Theologians name this divine indwelling "uncreated grace," precisely because it is the presence within the soul of grace's Author, the great Creator himself. Thus St. Alphonsus could write: "He who bears God in his heart, carries his paradise wherever he goes." Many celebrated mystics, notably St. Elizabeth of the Trinity, made this profound truth the master-light of their contemplative union with God.

Defending the Kingdom's Treasures

Along with the presence of the King comes a sharing in his own divine life; we call it "created grace." Being what it is, grace is full of splendours and wonders, all of which are in reality so many effects or reflections within the human soul of the indwelling Godhead. As to how inestimably precious grace is in itself, St. Thomas has this to say: "The entire material universe and everything it contains is of less value in God's eyes than the grace present in any individual person."

Through grace we equivalently become princes and princesses of God's kingdom and are endowed with its treasures. On that account we should ever heed Our Lord's warning to be on guard against sin's moths and thieves that threaten our priceless possession. St. Paul issues a similar warning, reminding us that we carry the kingdom's treasures in that fragile, brittle earthenware which is ourselves (cf. 2 Cor 4: 7). He further warns us against the wiles of the fallen angels; they who made shipwreck of their own destiny now continue their rebellion against the God of grace by doing their utmost to diminish if not actually destroy the grace of God present in his adopted sons and daughters (cf. Eph 6: 12).

The Church too is well aware of our need to guard the treasures of the kingdom entrusted to us. "Heavenly Father," runs a liturgical prayer, "by your constant care protect the good you have given us."

Growth in Grace and Holiness

Being a form of created life---indeed, the highest form possible---grace is a dynamic, not static, reality and consequently seeks of its very nature to grow and develop. Accordingly St. Paul emphasizes our obligation to promote this process, which he refers to as "the growth of the inner man" (cf. Eph 3:14-19). What spiritual growth basically implies is that, the more we respond to God's love, the more he fills us with his life-giving grace.

St. Peter too exhorts us "to grow up in grace" (2 Pet 3: 18). And John the Baptist supplied us with a classic formula to the effect that Christ must increase and we must decrease; which implies that the growth of grace automatically brings about the diminishment of sinful self-love (cf. Jn 3: 30). Each time, then, we pray "Thy kingdom come" we are primarily asking the God of grace to promote the vital growth-process within ourselves and others.

Because grace is essentially sanctifying, its principal product is holiness. And to aim at holiness is a divine command, since God himself is all-holy (cf. Lev.11: 22). Now the sure measure of holiness is the love we show God and our neighbour. And this is reflected in the fact that the saints were such maestros at loving God and their fellow-men with their entire heart, mind, soul and strength (cf. Mt 22: 37). In other words, they fulfilled to an heroic degree the Master's injunction to seek first the kingdom of God and his holiness (cf. Mt 6: 33).

Love is Anti-Sin

The primacy of love in the interior kingdom of God was well expressed by Pope Leo XIII. "The reign of Jesus Christ," he wrote, "takes its power and its quality from divine charity. To live holily and with right order is its foundation and perfection."

Because it is an imperative of God's kingdom that we be holy, our further obligation is to renounce anything sinful and give the God of the commandments top priority in all things. That is why so many masters of the spiritual life recommend that we make frequent acts of contrition and go regularly to Confession. G.M. Hopkins gave poetic expression to this department of the holiness programme:

> "There is your world within.
> There rid the dragons, root out there the sin.
> Your will is law in that small commonweal."

St. Cyril of Jerusalem is one of many who stress how essential a clean conscience is to the inward kingdom's wellbeing. Quoting St. Paul's injunction not to let sin reign in our mortal bodies, he declares that only those should presume to pray "Thy kingdom come" who have first purified themselves in thought, word and action.

Further Riches of the Kingdom

We saw earlier that God's interior kingdom is really an all-inclusive label for the many endowments he makes us, paramount among which are grace and charity. The list of endowments is long and impressive, including what are technically known as the theological virtues plus the sevenfold gifts and twelvefold fruits of the Holy Spirit. The overall purpose of these multiple gifts and powers is to equip us to live and function in the supernatural order to which we have been raised.

Add to this equipment the multitudinous actual graces that play about us all day and every day, bringing God's light and help into every corner of our personal inward world. And this inward world, as we are well aware, is a kaleidoscopic and ever-shifting pattern of thoughts and desires, memories and imaginations, hopes and anxieties, fears and ambitions, joys and sorrows, good resolutions and temptations, modest strivings after holiness, and the unremitting downward drag of our fallen human nature.

Unfortunately the limited compass of these pages does not allow us to look separately at each of the kingdom's splendid endowments, some of which are enumerated in the preface for Christ the King. Prominent among the gifts of the kingdom are faith, hope, life, holiness, justice, love and peace. And there are many others besides, including such substantial items as patience, joy and fear of the Lord.

Two Choice Treasures

Suffice it here to treat briefly of two of these kingdom-related gifts which, by reason of their all-important functions, merit a brief consideration. The first is faith. Its genius is that it gives us an overall vision, albeit shadowy and fitful, of the supernatural realities comprising the kingdom. Thanks to faith we can say with Francis

Thompson (significantly, he was speaking of the kingdom of God), "O world invisible, we view thee." The truly wonderful benefit brought by faith is that not only the kingdom and its treasures but the King himself fall within its purview. This applies very directly to his true presence in the Eucharist.

To sharpen our vision and give it an ever-clearer focus, we should often ask the God-Man, as did the apostles on one recorded occasion, "Lord, increase our faith" (Lk 17: 5). As it is, each time we pray "Thy kingdom come" we are also implicitly asking, among other things, for our faith-vision to be strengthened.

The second of God's gifts to merit special consideration is hope. Its whole secret is that it not only looks ahead to things future and longed-for but, relying on the divine goodness and help, confidently expects to obtain them, provided we ourselves do what in us lies. Hope could be called the virtue of great expectations. Its highest and noblest function in God's interior kingdom is to foster our longing and yearning for the Heaven-kingdom over time's horizon. "Thy eternal and glorious kingdom come" is what hope essentially has in mind each time we recite the Lord's prayer. "Maranatha: come Lord Jesus!" For the early Christians this was a fervent prayer and a waking dream, and we do well to follow their example.

The Church is God's Kingdom

That first-ever Pentecost Sunday in Jerusalem was the Church's birthday. For on that day it was launched into history under the action of the Holy Spirit. As for the rushing wind, it has ever since served to power the Church's onward momentum as it spans the centuries between Pentecost and Parousia. Only when its Founder returns in his glory will the Church's marathon pilgrimage and task be over. Then its members will rejoice for ever in God's heavenly kingdom, thanks to the ministrations they received during their pilgrim-days from his Church-kingdom.

Herein lies the Church's whole point and purpose. It is

God's temporal, visible kingdom, founded and structured to produce and promote his divine treasures in human souls. Thus the Church-kingdom, being the depository of the truths of revelation and the sacramental system, as well as being armed with sacred authority and forever sustained by the Holy Spirit, is well equipped to service and prepare its members for the kingdom's definitive, glorious stage in the eternal world following the resurrection.

Thus, in relation to its heavenly successor, the Church-kingdom, like the interior one, is intermediate, embryonic, preparatory. Nevertheless it is absolutely indispensable. Without it we would be poor and wretched indeed. Especially when we reach death's door we shall have occasion to be grateful and rejoice, as did St. Teresa of Avila, that we are members of God's one, holy, Catholic and apostolic Church.

More About the Church-Kingdom

The Church is rich in paradox. Being a human society, it is visible and external; yet at the same time it is divine, inasmuch as it is animated and powered by the invisible Spirit of God. Again, the Church is a world-wide organisation under the direction of a hierarchy led by the successor of St. Peter; yet it is equally an organism, a mystical body into which its members are incorporated through grace under Christ its Head.

Yet another paradox is that, on the one hand, the Church is the immaculate spouse of the Lamb, holy in its Founder and Head, holy in the indwelling Spirit of God, holy in its doctrine, in its sacraments, and in its many members already blessed in Heaven. On the other hand, every member of the Church, Christ's holy mother excepted, is at least to some degree sinful and in need of God's pardon.

What, we may well ask, is the Church's overriding responsibility and concern? The answer, as we would expect, is: the wellbeing of God's kingdom within its members. The state of their faith is a leading priority; which led St. Augustine to conclude that the Church-kingdom on earth is nothing else than the worldwide community of believers.

Prayer is another priority, it being our vital link not with God alone but with all members of the communion of saints. For the Church-kingdom continues to embrace its former members in Heaven and Purgatory alike. And through prayer we still on earth can join hands and exchange spiritual gifts with our fellow-members on both sides of death's divide. Newman understood this principle well. "He who attempts to set up God's kingdom in his heart," he wrote, "furthers it in the world."

When we pray "Thy kingdom come" we are further asking our heavenly Father to bless and prosper the Church's saving mission to mankind. In performing that mission it encounters much opposition and has to carry many a cross. Indeed, its entire history is virtually a way of the cross, so multiple have been the trials and persecutions it has had to endure. Yet this should not surprise us. After all, the Church-kingdom is doing God's work in a fallen world, with fallen angels obstructing it in every possible way with bitter and non-stop opposition.

Finally, let us reflect with St. Bernard that it glorifies and pleases the God of the kingdom when we offer his Church our filial love and undivided loyalty. St. Teresa of Avila was an outstanding example of the former quality; her love for the Church, its faults and failings notwithstanding, was ardent and unwavering. As for loyalty to the Church, St. Ignatius Loyola exemplifies this quality; his exhortation for us to "think with the Church" requires that we offer God, teaching and governing us through his earthly representatives, the homage of our mind and understanding together with our total obedience.

Church Unity

A defining characteristic or mark of Christ's Church is its unity. It is a kingdom united in faith, worship, sacraments and membership.

And Our Lord made clear that this unity must not only reflect the intimate unity between himself and his fellow-Persons in the Trinity but should seek to embrace our separated brethren who bear his name (cf. Jn 14: 20; Jn 17: 11).

The unity theme is most relevant at the start of the third millennium, and accordingly features prominently in Pope John Paul II's document on the subject. He recommends that, because the Jubilee Year provides Christians of all communions (Catholic, Protestant and Orthodox) with a common cause for rejoicing in the Saviour's 2000th birthday, they should make the dawn of the new millennium a time for fresh ecumenical initiatives and added ecumenical prayer. "We are to look together to the one Lord," he exhorts us, "in accordance with his prayer for unity."

Here the Holy Father is taking up the initiative set by Vatican II. It lamented the tragic divisions in Western Christendom at the time of the Reformation, divisions for which both sides share the blame for so wounding Christ's mystical body, the Church. The same applies to the earlier and no-less-tragic split of the Eastern and Western branches of Christendom. Both these major religious upheavals branded the second millennium as one of fragmentation and division. "Such wounds," the Council affirms, "contradict the will of Christ and are the cause of scandal to the world."

But the Pope's Jubilee Year perspective is not confined to the world of Christendom. Because the 2000th birthday of Christ is a time of celebration and divine grace for all mankind, he further urges us to extend the hand of fellowship and collaboration to our brothers and sisters in the non-Christian world---whether they be Jewish, Muslim, Hindu, Buddhist or anything else. To increase awareness of "our mutual journey to the Father," we must do what we can to foster with them an inter-religious dialogue based on profound mutual respect and understanding.

Christ the King

We gain many a fresh insight into the kingdom of God when viewed in the radiance streaming from the Light of the World---Christ the King of kings and Lord of lords. His kingly status and destiny were emblazoned across his life all the way from Nazareth to Golgotha; that is, from his conception in Mary's womb as the messianic descendant of King David to the inscription atop his cross and his moving dialogue with the repentant thief.

Of Christ's gospel message the core theme was the kingdom of God. Time and again, and in parable after parable, he outlined its nature and underlined its urgency. In addition, he clearly indicated the kingdom's threefold function---invisible within human souls, visible and operative as the universal sacrament of salvation, and culminating in beatitude without end in the post-Parousia world.

But there is yet another dimension to the Saviour's royal role. Over and above proclaiming, founding, sanctifying, governing the kingdom and pledging to bring it to its end-phase and fulfillment, He *is* the kingdom. Or to use an expression current in the early Church, the God-Man is the *autobasileia*; that is, in himself and of himself he personifies the kingdom of God and, at each of its three levels, is the embodiment of all its virtues and values.

Thus we who possess God's interior kingdom can say with St. Paul: "I live, no, not I, but Christ lives within me" (Gal 2: 20). And again with St. Paul we can identify the suffering Christ with our fellow-members of the Church who suffer hardship, pain, or persecution. As for the third manifestation of God's kingdom, Christ, being himself the Resurrection and the Life, will fill it with his own heavenly glory.

Our Eucharistic King

This mystery of Jesus as the personification of God's threefold kingdom takes on a still sharper focus and added immediacy in the light shed upon it by the Eucharist. Because the Word Incarnate is truly and substantially present in our tabernacles, it follows that it is from there he exercises throughout the entire kingdom his royal powers and prerogatives. Vatican II recognized this in declaring that the Eucharist contains the Church's entire spiritual wealth. And for this same reason we speak of Our Lord's kingdom as being Eucharistic.

This explains why Eucharistic devotions are so effective in promoting the growth of God's kingdom within us and in the Church. In fact, the tabernacle is equivalently what Scripture terms "the throne of grace" where God dispenses special favours to those who approach him humbly and confidently (cf. Heb 4: 16).

These favours are dispensed all the more liberally by our Eucharistic King when we approach him with a pure heart. For, like the Knights of the Round Table, we must ever "reverence our King as if he were our conscience, and our conscience as our King."

The following inspiring formula was framed by an early Church Council: "There is not, there never has been, and there never will be, a single human being for whom Christ did not suffer." Hereby we are reminded that zeal for souls is another issue especially dear to the Eucharistic Heart of our King.

For Charles Wesley the salvation of souls became a burning passion. "The arms of love that compass me," he wrote, "would all mankind embrace...Oh that all might catch the flame!" It was the fire of divine love cast on the earth by the Son of God that he yearned to see kindled in his fellow-men. A like zeal, in combination with strong patriotism, later inspired G.M. Hopkins to write:

> "Our King back, oh, upon English souls!
> More brightening her, rare-dear Britain,
> As his reign rolls."

The Heaven-Kingdom

Every time we say to the Father, "Thy kingdom come," we implicitly focus our faith and feast our hope on what St. Bernard calls "that city yet to come, the object of our quest." It is the Heaven-kingdom, the climax and full realization of the messianic kingdom launched into human history by the God-Man. And when history reaches its terminus with his second coming in glory to judge all mankind, he will inaugurate his kingdom's final paradisal stage.

What this entails is that our reassembled body-souls will share in the risen King's own resurrection perfections and beauty---as Mary already does, in recognition of and reward for her unique supporting role in her Son's redemptive mission. Moreover, and as Scripture promises, this material world of ours will likewise be transfigured as part of the renewal of all things (cf. Rom 8: 19-23). Thereafter the elect citizens of the Heaven-kingdom will enjoy the Beatific Vision without end in their sublime future habitat, "the new heavens and the new earth" (2 Pet 3: 13).

There is surely no article of the creed that presents us with a scenario more momentous, awesome, dramatic and exciting than does the end of this world and the beginning of the brave new world to come. However, let us never forget that for every individual one of us the Judgment Day scenario will also be critical---in the literal sense of this word. For when divine judgment has been executed upon each single human being, the Judge's angels will duly separate the sheep from the goats, the wheat from the weeds. It should therefore be our daily and earnest concern to make ourselves eligible for eventual admission into Christ's eternal kingdom; the required criteria are crystal-clear from the inspired pages of Scripture and the Church's teaching.

Strengthening our Hope

Meanwhile our Christian hope gives us firm confidence that we will safely attain our heavenly destiny. To this end St. John Vianney offers us a practical and helpful formula." If I make the good God reign in my heart," he says, "he will make me reign with him in his glory."

Now, as is widely recognized, the most effective way to make and maintain God's reign in our heart is devotion to the Eucharist. What is more, the Eucharist is specifically designed to fortify our faith in the risen world to come. For the Eucharistic Jesus has himself assured us that his own risen body is the pledge and pattern of our own bodily resurrection (cf. Jn 6: 53-55). Furthermore, the Eucharistic mysteries, we are reminded by Pope John Paul II, besides uniting us with the heavenly liturgy and thus helping us anticipate eternal life, are "an ongoing proclamation of Christ's glorious second coming at the end of time."

Loving the Kingdom

Meanwhile, each passing day brings us closer to what Tennyson described as "the one far-off divine event to which the whole creation moves." In fact, we do not know how far-off or proximate the Parousia-event will be. All that we are certain about is that it will one day come, bringing human history to its grand finale and leading in the new order of paradisal glory for the elect. Christ will then deliver the kingdom over to his and our eternal Father.

"Almighty God," the Church prays in the Common of Holy Women, "may we burn with love for your kingdom." Here the Church is asking for a grace many of us stand in need of--- particularly as regards the glorious kingdom ahead. In addition to fostering the kingdom within us, this grace of loving the kingdom will stir our zeal for souls, precious souls for whom the Son of God bled to death so that they might participate in his resurrection and share his glory in our Father's abode.

This same grace will also help us meet the temptation to become over-attached to this-worldly realities as if they were permanent and definitive. Here on earth we have no abiding city but look for one to come (cf. Heb 13: 14). Love of the kingdom will further inspire us to recognise and look forward eagerly to "our true homeland in Heaven" (Phil 3: 20).

Chapter FIVE

THE GOD WHO RULES

"The devil plotted since the world began,
With alchemies of fire and witch's oil
And magic, but he never made a man.
I tell you every soul is great."

For our world so recently embarked on the third Christian millennium, and so much in need of God's guidance in planning and building the new civilization of love, Chesterton's lines come as a gift from Heaven. For they highlight a truth lying at the very heart of the Christian vision: namely, every single one of the six billion human beings currently on board planet earth is the Creator's special handiwork; each is a masterpiece, unique of its kind, that out-values all else in the material world. So valuable indeed are we human creatures in God's eyes that "the most worthless of us is of eternal worth."

Every soul is great because, being gifted with rational intelligence and free will, all of us are images---each in his own distinctive, inimitable way---of the Creator. Also, and for the same reason, we are spirits, albeit embodied ones, and as such are immortal; that is, an eternal future awaits us beyond death's horizon. To be more exact, two alternative futures await us, one of everlasting life, the other of everlasting death. Graham Greene referred to these as "the two eternities."

Every soul is great for the further reason that human wills wield the awesome power---and corresponding responsibility---of deciding for themselves which of the two eternities will be their final dwelling-place. Each man's free will, and it alone, makes that final and fateful decision. To be sure, God's grace floods him all along life's road with helps and warnings and inspirations; but ultimately it rests with the individual to take that definitive and irreversible step into destiny or disaster. Thus to the very end of his mortal days, and out beyond into eternity, man, great man, remains what God made him---"the captain of his fate, the master of his soul."

God's Will and Ours

Every soul is great for yet another and wholly sublime reason: the Incarnate Son of God, knowing the supreme value of souls, has paid with his very lifeblood for their redemption. Yet the Creator never revokes his gift of free will; accordingly, each person must decide for himself whether or not to accept and cooperate with divine grace ever knocking at his door. This choice, which faces us repeatedly every day of our lives, is a stark one, and never more so than at our final hour. "See," says the Lord, "I have set before thee this day a choice between life and death, between good fortune and ill" (Deut 30: 15).

St. Augustine coined a classic formula to express the mystery of God's will interacting with our own: "He who created us without our help will not save us without our consent." Nor in the meantime will God even sanctify us without our consent. In other words, his grace never coerces our freedom. Far from being a tyrant or despot, God is a loving Father who never violates the gift of free choice with which he has ennobled his children.

Certainly the divine will is that we be progressively sanctified and finally saved (cf. I Thess 4: 3; 1 Tim 2: 4). But the indispensable precondition is that our wills must first surrender to God's. The pattern for this was set by Our Lord during his Gethsemane agony: "Not my will but thine be done" (Lk 22: 42). And matching this is the petition in the Lord's Prayer: "Thy will be done on earth as it is in Heaven"

Discerning God's Will

How, then, are we to discern God's will in order to fulfil it? The answer is that it reaches us in a variety of ways, which may loosely be likened to a series of wavelengths. First of these is the decalogue. Comprising the equivalent of our Maker's instructions, his ten commandments brief us very explicitly on our basic religious and moral duties.

A second wavelength bringing us the divine will is the Church's teaching. "He who hears you," said Our Lord to his apostles, "hears me" (Lk 10: 16). Hence the Apostolic Church, armed with its Founder's authority and teaching commission, commands our obedience, more especially regarding defined doctrines as well as definitive ones. Similarly the Church's moral teaching calls for our compliance, since it expresses God's will concerning human behaviour.

It is in the intimacy of our world within that we act as receivers for a third wavelength communicating God's will. We call it conscience, which Newman hails as "a messenger from him who in nature and in grace speaks to us behind a veil." He says further: "Conscience is the true vicar of Christ in the soul: a prophet in its information; a monarch in its peremptoriness; a priest in its blessings and anathemas, according as we obey or disobey it."

Being in effect God's voice within us, conscience speaks with his own authority. And the imperative underlying its every injunction is: whatever the cost, obey the divine will in all things and at all times. To ensure that we get its message, this unsleeping voice by turns warns us, reminds us, nags us, reproaches us, torments us, counsels us, prompts us, urges us, encourages us. Sweetest of all, conscience rewards us with that only peace which flows from the uniting of our will with the Father's. Dante knew about this; hence his saying: "In God's will lies our peace."

Vatican II upheld conscience as "a man's most secret core and sanctuary; there he is alone with God, whose voice echoes in his depths." Without fail, then, we should be alert and sensitive to every instruction and warning whispered within us by the Spirit of God---the Spirit whose will is identical with that of our heavenly Father.

God in Life's Circumstances

There is yet another important wavelength God our Father uses for transmitting his holy will to his children. It can be described as the general framework in which he as our Creator has set our lives. Thus in his providential designs each individual is born of certain parents at a certain time in a certain place and within a certain cultural milieu; besides, he inherits certain genetic elements that largely determine what he is physically, mentally and psychologically.

All these antecedent circumstances, through being predetermined and completely outside our control, are to that extent fixed and unchangable. And, notwithstanding their inevitable flaws and inadequacies, we must humbly accept these circumstances as a gift coming from the hand of our all-good Creator. For they form that basic framework in which he wills us to serve him in this world and work out our salvation.

But as regards what is served up to us by this world, it is anything but fixed and unchangeable. For life is a quick-change artist that can produce without a moment's notice the most unpredictable happenings and circumstances. The result is that life's scenarios are liable to change, sometimes rapidly and even radically. Nevertheless we must learn to recognize and revere God's will beneath and behind everything life deals out to us. "He fixed thee midst this dance of plastic circumstance." And he did so, Browning explains, in order to shape us more and more perfectly after the pattern his providence intends.

The Problem of Evil

Unhappily, though, life's ever-changing circumstances are liable to include things like pain, suffering, failure, disappointment, tragedies, accidents, natural disasters---the catalogue is endless. Whence two questions naturally arise: how are we to reconcile evils like these with God's goodness and providence? And how can we ascribe such unwanted and painful things to his merciful will?

The solution is that, to be sure, God's absolute will embraces the totality of things. Some of these, however, come to pass only through what is known as his permissive will. Thus man, self-determining man, remains free to abuse his free will by breaking the commandments. Thus, too, hurtful things are allowed by God to occur in the physical order, especially if natural laws are flouted. In any case, the physical order, for all its regularity, wonder and beauty, is finite and therefore limited and inherently fragile. So things unfortunately can and sometimes do go wrong---and to our cost.

St. Paul supplies us with a key text to reassure us that, whatever physical or moral evils come to overshadow our lives, God's will for us remains positive, constructive, sanctifying, even consoling. "Everything that happens," the text in question reads, "works together for the good of those who love God, those whom he has called in fulfillment of his design" (Rom 8: 28).

What these words tell us is that the alchemy of love can transmute into the gold of grace every cross and trial life may come up with---if we accept them as gifts, for such they are, coming with God's permission and loving purpose into our lives. What is still more wonderful, even past repented sins, paradoxical though this may seem, can in the designs of providence become for us so many stepping-stones to a higher and closer union with the all-forgiving Father.

Sacrament of the Present Moment

Next to consider what is in effect a fine-tuned, hi-fi version of the wavelength we have just been considering. And what makes this advanced version so special is that it transforms each passing moment of our lives into a carrier of the Father's will. That is to say, each present moment, whatever it may bring into our lives, is seen as a meeting-point where human wills encounter the Creator's.

"Thy will be done" is the refrain running through the succession of passing moments, transfiguring them into messengers and bearers of something specially foreseen and planned by God. Now it is a duty to be performed, now a cross to be endured, now a joy to be embraced---the things providence brings into our lives are many and varied. But, whatever form they take, we are to grasp and kiss the Father's hand that proffers them. So it comes about that, by uniting ourselves in this manner with his will, we become pliable instruments for carrying out his holy purposes.

It was the French Jesuit, Jean-Pierre de Caussade, who did much to popularize this method of establishing union with the divine will. "What happens each moment," he explains, "bears the imprint of the will of God. It is by union with his will that we enjoy and possess him, and it is an illusion to endeavour to obtain this divine enjoyment by any other means. If we understood how to see in each moment some manifestation of the will of God, we should also find therein everything that our hearts could desire."

The God of Providence

As we have been seeing, the will of God is all-embracing, powerful, providential, caring, kind. Every single thing that happens falls within the ambit of the Almighty's all-seeing knowledge and providence and can be made to work for our good. Consequently nothing can be attributed to mere chance or pure coincidence. "Chance," to quote a wise and witty French proverb, "is a nickname we give to providence." As for coincidence, Pope John Paul II among others assures us that "it has no part in the plans of divine providence."

A further wise counsel was expressed by St. Peter. "Throw

back on God," he says, "the burden of all your anxiety; he is concerned for you" (1 Pet 5: 7). Now a frequent source of anxiety affecting a good many people is the future as such, the unknown, frowning future. Will they, they wonder, be able to cope with what lies in the days and months ahead? The remedy against all future-related fears and concerns is to place our trust absolutely in the God of providence.

The words of Newman's hymn about this are designed to calm our anxieties like gentle music, reassuring us that the kindly light of the Father's providence will lead us on securely and unerringly through whatever gloom or darkness may envelop us. Nor do we wish to see the distant scene; one step at a time is enough, knowing as we do that the firm hand leading us on is the Lord's.

A More Particular Providence

There is yet another wavelength along which the Father's will is conveyed to a certain privileged elite. It is the exquisitely sensitive rule he exercises over those who have consecrated their lives to his service in religious life. What this consecration involves, among other things, is that men and women religious are obliged by their vow of obedience to obey the superiors placed over them. And they must do so, St. Ignatius teaches, not because their superiors happen to be wise or prudent or anything else, but simply and solely because they hold the place of God. For it is his divine authority that underlies not just obedience but the entire infrastructure of religious life. Thus St. Margaret Mary could instruct her novices: "The way of God for us is by our holy rules."

G.M. Hopkins applied the expression "lovely-felicitous providence" to God's solicitous rule over those bound to him by vows. He further said: "When a man has given himself to God's service, when he has denied himself and followed Christ, he has fitted himself to receive from God a special guidance, a more particular providence. This guidance is conveyed partly by the action of other men, as his appointed superiors, and partly by direct lights and inspirations."

Faithful to the End

In one of her liturgical prayers the Church addresses God as follows: "Father of all that is good, keep us faithful in serving you, for to serve you is our lasting joy." Faithfulness in serving God is, in fact, much the same thing as faithfulness to his will. And to keep on being faithful is a lifelong task for everyone. Pope Paul VI formulated this truth in a novel way when addressing a group of elderly French pilgrims. "There is no retirement age," he said, "from accomplishing God's will, which is that we become saints."

Faithfulness connotes that one is loyal, reliable, constant, trustworthy, dependable, steadfast, persevering---these and other qualities besides. Above all, the faithful servant is devoted to his duty, be it to God, his neighbour, or his state of life. Why duty is so sacred is because the divine will is enshrined within it; consequently duty's faithful performance is the sure path to sanctification, peace of soul, and final salvation.

Faithful perseverance in doing one's duty also calls for much patience. And this we have to practise literally on a daily basis. For that is how life deals with us here on earth; as a saying attributed to Fulton Sheen puts it, God gives us life on the instalment plan---one day at a time.

A further difficulty to be faced is that so much of daily life and the performance of duty can become dull, stale and monotonous through being repetitive and boring. And this can duly tempt us to grow "weary of well doing," as St. Paul warns (2 Thess 3: 13). To counter this we should unite ourselves frequently with the heavenly Father, whose will we have made into the lodestar of our lives, and whose kindly providence presides over everything we are and everything we do.

So it comes about that faithfulness to duty casts a halo around the humdrum and sheds the glow of God's love over the most drab and commonplace of routines. As St. Teresa of Avila once remarked, faith can see God walking among the pots and pans as surely as he did in the garden of Eden. This further goes to explain why, like that of many another saint, her devotion was strongly drawn to the Holy House of Nazareth. For there, amid domestic realities of the most ordinary kind, the Eternal Father's will was enthroned and perfectly executed in the everyday lives of Jesus, Mary and Joseph.

Jesus and His Father's Will

It was the Word made Flesh who taught us to say: "Thy will be done on earth as it is in Heaven." And so perfectly did he himself practise what he taught that he exemplified total and loving submission to the Father's will. "My meat and my drink," he declared, "is to do the will of him who sent me" (Jn 4: 34). Let us now look at the implications of this in the light that streams from the mystery of the Incarnation.

Our faith teaches us that Jesus is the God-Man. That is, he is the Second Person of the Trinity made man in order to be our Redeemer. Which means, as the Church has defined, that Christ has two natures, divine and human; and which further means that correspondingly he has two principles of operation and two wills.

Now these two wills were clearly never in opposition to each other. On the contrary, so perfectly united and cooperative were they that, as man, the Son of God, in obedience to his Father, willed humanly everything he himself had divinely decreed, jointly with the Father and the Holy Spirit, for man's salvation. For the three Divine Persons, let us recall, possess one and the same divine nature and therefore the identical mind and will.

"Lo, I have come to do your will, O God" (Heb 10: 7). This characterised the Incarnate Word's mission right from the outset. Also he attested that he always did what was pleasing to his Father (cf. Jn 8: 29). And it was at a defining moment in his life---the agony in the garden---that he made the supreme surrender of his human will to the divine, saying, "Not my will but thine be done" (Lk 22: 42).

St. Paul constantly refers to the humble sacrifice of Christ's human will to the divine as the very instrument of our redemption, as was the sacrifice of his all-too-human body on the cross (cf. Gal 1:4; Heb 10:10).

As it is in Heaven

Mary, the Queen of Heaven, remains what she was during her mortal days---the perfect instrument of the Father's will. All the way from her Fiat at Nazareth to the very end of her days, her spirit magnified the Lord by faultlessly carrying out his will. Indeed, she was the living embodiment and exemplar of the psalmist's prayer: "Now and ever to do thy will perfectly, O God, is my heart's aim" (Ps 118: 112).

Insofar as God's will is both source and goal of every grace we receive, she who "mothers every grace that does now reach our race" plays, by this same token, a vital role in the operations of God's will in our lives. She earnestly desires that we cherish it and embrace it as a treasure from Heaven. And, at a practical level, she passes on to us the same golden counsel she gave her Son's apostles at the Cana wedding-feast: "Do whatever he tells you" (Jn 2: 5).

As for the angelic inhabitants of heaven, they too are totally wedded to the will of our heavenly Father. This has been so ever since that fateful moment of truth and decision when, cooperating with God's grace, they chose to obey his will rather than join the renegade Lucifer and his followers in rebelling against divine authority.

As reward for their loyalty, God admitted those angels to the Beatific Vision and the glory of Heaven; now and forever they worship the Lord and, in Scripture's words, "wait on him like winds and flames of fire" (Heb 1: 7). This text refers to the services the angels render us on earth as our appointed guardians and helpers. St. Thomas sees the role of a guardian angel for each of us as "a particular application of divine providence." Significantly Our Lord himself testified that our guardians ceaselessly see the face of his Father in Heaven (cf. Mt 18: 10). From this it follows that their overriding and burning concern in our regard is that, like themselves, we serve the Father by doing his will always and in all things.

Artists of the Divine Will

In the second Eucharistic Prayer we address God the Father in these words: "Make us worthy to share eternal life with Mary...and with all the saints who have done your will throughout the ages."

The galaxy of God's holy ones in Heaven is almost mind-boggling to contemplate, so multitudinous are they and so richly varied in their human differences. But they evince one common defining characteristic: while on earth they loved God with every fibre of their being. And this love was fuelled by their passionate dedication to God's will.

This dedication it was that gave both direction and driving-power to their lives. As with their Master, it became meat and drink for them to comply lovingly with the Father's every instruction. They saw the hand of his providence in all things. Through their fine-tuned union with his will they raised holiness of life to an art form, distinguishing themselves as blue-ribbon performers in the divine service.

Every saint would fully endorse what one of their most illustrious members---the Curé d'Ars---said on this subject: "There is nothing so sweet, and nothing so perfect, as to do the will of God. In order to do things well, we must do them as God wills, in all conformity with his designs."

It is for our inspiration and imitation that the Church parades her saints before us. Henry Vaughan wrote in this connection:

> "God's saints are shining lights.
> They are indeed our pillar-fires
> Seen as we go.
> They are that City's shining spires
> We travel to."

As a help towards doing God's will more faithfully and fervently, let us look briefly at a handful of God's star performers selected at random from his galaxy of holy ones. To begin with St. Jean Frances de Chantal. She meant and lived every single syllable of her prayer: "O my God, may thy will be done in me, with no ifs, no buts, no exceptions." Equally earnest was St. Margaret Mary, that model of exact fidelity to the Holy Spirit's least whisper; one of her sayings was that "we must not belong to God by halves." As for Mother Teresa of Calcutta, we can discern what is virtually her self-portrait in the formula she coined: "True holiness consists in doing God's will with a smile."

Some More Artists

Well-known is St. Bernadette's remark made during her final days as an invalid: "The task God has given me is that of being ill." Furthermore, she saw this as a rich offering she could make to God for the conversion of sinners. She also described her new role as being Our Lady's broom standing idle and unused in a corner now that its former active role had been accomplished. In this we are reminded of St. Theresa of Lisieux likening herself to a handball or plaything in the hands of the Infant Jesus.

Inspiring too was the example of Blessed Damien of Molokai; he remained not only calm and resigned but radiantly happy when he contracted leprosy from those he was caring for. Two things, he testified, kept him going on his hard and difficult road. One was his daily Holy Hour before the Blessed Sacrament. The other was, in his own words: "I daily repeat from my heart,'Thy will be done.'"

It has been said of Blessed Padre Pio that he revered the will of God as a sacrament of sanctification and peace. As for the great Cardinal Newman, so renowned for his holiness and learning, divine providence would subsequently take him at his word when he addressed this prayer to the Father: "I am born to serve you, to be your instrument."

More recent instruments in the hands of divine providence were Blessed Faustina Kowalska and Blessed Gianna Molla. The former reveals in her diary the importance God attaches to our absolute fidelity in adhering to his will; also, how divinely merciful his will is, being indeed identical with his love. The story of Blessed Gianna Molla is that of a radiant and ardently devout young Italian doctor who sacrificed her own life for the safe delivery of her third child. Till the very painful end she remained unshakeably united with the will of the eternal Father.

As a final example of heroic sanctity embracing God's will, there is the sublime self-sacrifice of St. Maximilian Kolbe in Auschwitz death-camp. Not long before the end he wrote to his mother: "God is everywhere; he watches with great love over all and everything." By offering to die in place of a fellow-prisoner, St. Maximilian emulated his Master's obedience to the Father's will in being prepared to die on behalf of others. Like his Master again, said Pope Paul VI, the saint humbly consented "to be expiation, to be victim, to be sacrifice, and finally to be love."

The Holy Spirit's Gifts

The Father's will for each of us, let it be recalled, has one overriding aim---our sanctification and salvation. And to this end he has supplied us with a whole array of supernatural endowments, among which are the so-called sevenfold gifts of the Holy Spirit. Each of these contributes in its own way towards our more perfect receptiveness to the divine will and our implementation of its behests.

Now to consider briefly the main functions and effects of the Holy Spirit's gifts in helping us obey and carry out the Father's will. Piety warms our filial love towards him and kindles zeal for all his holy purposes. Besides deepening our trust in divine providence, piety moves us to imitate the Virgin Mary, the angels and the saints in loving and honouring the will that rules Heaven and earth.

The gift of knowledge guides our minds to see and evaluate all things in relation to their Creator. In this present context, knowledge focuses on his absolute authority over all his creatures---beginning with ourselves. And in its light we clearly perceive, as did the psalmist, how very frail and inconstant are our wills (cf. Ps 34: 4).

Furthermore, knowledge enlightens us to perceive more clearly that the underlying cause of this frailty and inconstancy is original sin and its effects. All can identify one hundred per cent with St. Paul when he admits: "My own actions bewilder me; what I do is not what I wish to do, but something which I hate...If what I do is something I have no wish to do, my action does not come from me but from the sinful principle that dwells in me...It is not the good my will prefers, but the evil my will disapproves, that I find myself doing...Inwardly I applaud God's disposition, but I observe another disposition in my lower self, which raises war against the disposition of my conscience" (Rom 7: 15-17,19, 23).

Our Sinful Wills

St. Paul is almost saying that original sin has made split personalities of us. That is, two selves are in perpetual conflict within us---the higher that approves and welcomes the designs of God's will, the lower that opposes and rejects them. Anyhow, it is our free will, wounded and weakened by original sin, that is the main culprit when we flout divine commands. No one was more aware of this than St. Augustine; hence his dictum: "It is the will that sins." He means hereby that our every offence against God's will, whatever its nature, is motivated and powered by our sin-inclined will.

"Know thyself." The ancient adage plays its part in the gift of knowledge, exposing the fault line located in the human will. This helps greatly to explain why sometimes we are apt to be unsubmissive, rebellious, wayward, resistant, stubborn and worse in our relations with the divine will as made known to us. Knowledge not only helps us to see this situation clearly; it perceives equally clearly the great strength and protection ever available from the God of divine grace if we call upon him.

The gift known as fear of the Lord acts as a powerful brake on our innate tendencies towards wilful self-love and defiance of God's will. Fear of the Lord's main operation lies in appealing to us to continue being obedient children of our heavenly Father; at the same time it generates a profound respect for the divine law's imperatives and sanctions. This gift's core message is: "Bow down before the mighty hand of God" (I Pet 5: 6). But do so, the message further implies, not as cowed slaves but as cherished children fearful of offending such a good Father in Heaven.

Counsel and Fortitude

St. Paul repeatedly enjoins us to seek and choose God's will, which he once alluded to as "the good thing, the desirable thing, the perfect thing" (Rom 12: 2). But this seeking and choosing can give rise to problems, particularly when a hard decision has to be made between alternative options, and even more particularly when the decision affects other people's lives, as is the case in governance and spiritual direction. In all such situations the gift of counsel proves invaluable, thanks to the help we receive from the Holy Spirit in making the right choice---the choice prompted and sanctified by the divine will.

Our final consideration is the gift of fortitude. Its role is to fortify our wayward wills when God permits difficulties, sufferings, sorrows, obstacles and other trials to come our way. Fortitude reaches its highest and noblest level in martyrdom, strengthening ordinary mortals even to welcome and caress their sufferings and death as a gift from the Father's permissive will. The martyrs see themselves as privileged sharers in what their Master underwent on Good Friday. With wonderful bravery they embrace the Father's will and go out like conquering heroes to their eternal reward.

This is the so-called martyrdom of blood. But there is another and less spectacular form of martyrdom that equally relies on fortitude to help it scale the heights of holiness. Pope John Paul II speaks of it as "the martyrdom of illness, weakness and infirmity." Those called by God to be martyrs of this kind equally qualify as heroes of the divine will by co-suffering with Christ on behalf of his mystical body, the Church (cf. Col 1:24). And in the process they achieve the closest union with him whose fatherly will must at all costs be done on earth as it is in Heaven.

Chapter SIX

THE GOD WHO PROVIDES

Always a most pleasing sight to behold is that of broad and smiling wheatfields on a summer's day. There they stretch out before you in the sunshine, ripe with the promise of harvest, swaying and rippling in the breeze like waves on a golden sea. And one's thoughts rise spontaneously in praise and thanksgiving to the Creator. For it is to him that we owe this good earth, this bountiful earth, which so faithfully produces, year after year, "bread to sustain our bodies and wine to cheer our hearts" (Ps 103:13-15).

In giving thanks to the Creator we are at the same time acknowledging him as the God of providence; which literally means he provides us with our essential needs for life's journey. And of these needs none is more essential than daily food for bodily life and sustenance. Which truism happens incidentally to be highlighted in the rousing chorus about "food, glorious food" in the musical *Oliver*.

More importantly, our essential need for food is highlighted in the Lord's Prayer. Its Author, with a first-hand knowledge of human nature to draw upon, was deeply aware of our material requirements, paramount among which is bodily nourishment. Accordingly he taught us to draw it to our Father's attention as a top-priority issue. Thus we pray: "Give us this day our daily bread."

Bread's Wider Meaning

Certainly of all articles of food the most universal, familiar and basic is bread. So much so, indeed, that in biblical usage bread often stands not only for food as such but for all our earthly necessities. Thus we find St. Thomas, in line with tradition, confirming this usage in his commentary on the Lord's Prayer: "The needs of this present life, for each individual according to his station, are expressed under the name of bread."

As for "our daily bread," the same tradition understands the phrase to include not only the bread which is Christ's Eucharistic body but the bread of God's word for our minds and hearts. We shall presently be looking more closely at these issues besides a number of others directly related to the theme. These related issues include the prayer of petition, the mystery of divine providence, and the natural solidarity that binds mankind into a world-wide human family.

Whence arises a further and vital issue facing the family of mankind so recently launched into the third millennium: namely, the challenge of building a new civilisation of love and justice on the foundation of the Father's truth and providence, a civilisation in which hunger has no place and all God's human images live in conditions consonant with their dignity.

The Prayer of Petition

In asking the Father for our daily bread, we are practising a form of prayer repeatedly recommended by Our Lord himself. "Ask and you shall receive," he invites us in the gospel (Mt 7: 7) And we are to ask the Father for whatever we like, notwithstanding the fact that he knows perfectly well in advance what our needs are (cf. Mt 6: 8).

To reinforce his lesson, Christ made the Lord's Prayer into what is in effect a tissue of petitions. In other words, every one of its seven parts expresses a specific desire or intention. And none is more specific than our request for daily bread, which in the context is a codeword for all our temporal needs.

"Anything that we lawfully desire may properly be asked of God in prayer." St. Augustine's formula indicates how wide a scope our petitions can cover. But what if our requests go unanswered? Or as a poet expressed it, "What if they meet with a brazen heaven?"

We should certainly not take this to mean that God is saying No; rather, as many authorities assure us, he may simply be deferring his Yes to a more opportune time. As the old adage counsels us, "God's delays are not God's denials." Also relevant here is the parable about the Unjust Judge, its whole point being that we should persevere untiringly in asking God to give us what we are asking (cf. Lk 18: 1-8).

Sometimes, however, God does say No to our requests, howsoever justified and deserving they may seem. But he does so because he foresees that sooner or later they would in fact work to our disadvantage. Shakespeare said in this regard:

> "We, ignorant of ourselves,
> Beg often our own harms, which the wise powers
> Deny us for our good. So find we profit
> By losing of our prayers."

God's Ways and Ours

We may rest assured, however, that God rewards our every prayer by granting us something very worthwhile, even if it is not the precise something we had in mind. A notable example was the worried St. Monica's prayer that her wayward son Augustine should not leave Carthage for Rome. But leave Carthage he did-and would thus in due course be led to meet St. Ambrose, the man destined by providence to influence his life so profoundly.

Another important point about the prayer of petition is that God is obviously more disposed to favour those who habitually seek his kingdom and do his will in all things. St. John was very explicit about this. "If conscience does not condemn us," he declares, "we can appear boldly before God, and he will grant all our requests, since we are keeping his commandments and living as he would see us live" (I Jn 3: 21-22).

Finally, and hardly necessary to point out, we should not ask God for things that are patently silly and impracticable. Origen supplies us with a hypothetical example; we should not, he says, petition God to give us the cool of spring at the height of summer. A further example of a semi-comic kind has been suggested by a modern author; we should not, he urges, petition God to grow cabbages on a patch of concrete.

Providence and Ourselves

In asking the Father to give us our daily bread, we are expressing our trust in his providence. And how vitally important this trust is has been underlined by many spiritual guides. St. Francis of Sales, for example, exhorts us: "Do not look ahead to what might happen tomorrow. The same everlasting Father who cares for you today will take care of you tomorrow and every day."

Providence implies that God presides over his entire creation, noting everything down to the tiniest detail and providing all creatures with what they need. It is by his wisdom, power and goodness, St. Augustine remarks, "that the world is governed, right down to the windblown leaves of the trees."

But the providential Father cares in an altogether special way for those whom he has fashioned in his own image and called to share his divine nature as adopted children (cf. Gen 1;17; 2 Pet 1:4). We see this reflected in Our Lord's constant focusing on the need for trust in the Father who makes his sun rise on the bad and the good, who sends rain on the just and the unjust, who feeds the birds of the air, and who adorns the flowers of the field so exquisitely. The Word Incarnate urges us to seek primarily the kingdom of God and his justice, promising that all else will be provided, thanks to our gracious and bountiful Father.

Christ also cautions us repeatedly against anxiety, over-solicitude and worry; which caution was later echoed by St. Peter: "Throw back on God the burden of all your anxiety; he is concerned for you" (1 Pet 5: 7). Similarly we find the Lord's cautioning words echoed in the Mass prayer that immediately follows the Our Father: "Lord, in your mercy free us from sin, and protect us from all anxiety, as we wait in joyful hope for the coming of our Saviour Jesus Christ."

Cooperating with Providence

But trust in the Lord and abandonment to his providence do not exclude due planning and work on our part. The Catholic Catechism makes clear that the Lord is not "inviting us to idleness" when he insists on our absolute trust in his Father's care. Yet at the same time he requires on our part a measure of collaboration. This is clearly demonstrated in the production of our daily bread; coming originally in the form of wheat as the Father's gift, it nonetheless postulates the cooperative efforts of sower, harvester and baker in order to become the finished product.

The danger lurking here is the sin of presumption. It neglects due effort on our part and expects providence to do everything. St. Ignatius has given us a fail-safe formula that strikes a balance between the divine and the human input in any enterprise on our part. "Pray," he counsels us, "as if everything depended on God, and work as if everything depended on yourself."

The same principle applies to God's providence over the animal and vegetable kingdom. He feeds the birds of the air, but not from the equivalent of a golden spoon. They must find the available food for themselves; and the mother-bird must bring it back to the nest to feed her hungry chicks.

As for the flowers of the field that neither reap nor spin nor gather into barns, and yet become so entrancingly lovely and fragrant, they too must contribute their effort to the providential process. They do so in the first place underground; that is, their roots constantly seek and absorb moisture and nourishment from the soil. Their cooperative activity also takes place above ground, where the plant draws in air and sunshine for its growth and development.

The Prayer of Thanksgiving

The first thing to be said in this context is that we should without fail thank God before and after every meal. This is a courtesy we owe in gratitude to him whose providence has gifted us so abundantly in the affluent West with "food, glorious food."

Not only food, however, calls for our regular prayer of thanksgiving. Literally everything we are and everything we have makes a like claim, since all derives ultimately from the Creator's goodness and bounty. "What have you got," St. Paul asks, "that you did not receive from God?" (1 Cor 4: 7). We acknowledge our debt of gratitude to him for the sum-total of his gifts every time we say in the Mass preface: "It is right and fitting that we should at all times and in all places give you thanks."

So the Lord's Prayer teaches us, among other things, to show deep gratitude to the "Giver of breath and bread" and of all else besides. In this respect the prayer of thanksgiving conforms to the pattern set by several Old Testament writers---King David in particular. "My soul," he says in his characteristic style, "give thanks to the Lord. All my being, bless his holy name. My soul, give thanks to the Lord, and never forget all his blessings" (Ps 102: 1-2).

Counting Our Blessings

"Never forget all his blessings"---the psalmist's exhortation recalls a eye-catching and thought-provoking slogan displayed on a signboard outside a church in central London. It read: "Counting your blessings is not an easy sum."

In point of fact, it is an impossible sum, since God's blessings are as numerous as flakes falling in a snowstorm. These blessings are brought into our lives by providence in two basic forms---material and spiritual. The material ones cover such data as who we are and what we are, our bodies, our particular talents, and the general setting and circumstances of our lives and our work.

As regards God's spiritual blessings, they are many and multiform. Leading the way is our being called into existence in the first place; which consideration drew St. Bernard's famous remark: "The first gift God gives me is myself." The second of God's all-precious gifts is our redemption from sin and damnation; so much does our Father love us and prize us that he allowed his Only-begotten to bleed to death on our behalf. A third priceless gift from our provident God is the Church, through whose agency we receive his further gift of faith and its revealed certitudes, plus the seven sacraments, preeminently the Eucharist.

Add to these spiritual blessings God's unique gift of Mary, the mother of Jesus, to be our mother also. In her role as Mediatrix of All Graces she dispenses the divine life to us in our every need, not least at that all-decisive moment when we make out exit from this world. Not to be omitted either from this selected list of spiritual blessings is the angel companion whom the God of providence has appointed to enlighten, guard, rule and guide each of us on our lifelong journey to the City of God.

So the Lord's Prayer serves to stir our gratitude and make us more keenly aware than ever that "every best gift and every perfect gift is from above, coming down from the Father of lights" (Jas 1:17). Chesterton summed up our situation admirably when we said: "We should take life with gratitude, not for granted."

Not Me but We

There is a deep significance in the word "our" qualifying the daily bread we request of God. Its function is to focus our charity and concern beyond the exclusive interests of "me" to the immensely wider world of "we." That is, the Lord's Prayer, here and in its other petitions, reaches out to and embraces nothing less than the world-wide human family, "the whole commonwealth of humanity," as Pius XII called it.

So the Our Father is really the prayer of human brotherhood under God. And it helps us to see, with G.M. Hopkins, that "every man is my mate and counterpart." At the natural level to begin with, human solidarity binds us together, whatever our ethnic, cultural and other differences. For, by the Creator's gracious providence, all national communities come from the identical primogenitors and share a common nature and destiny. And meanwhile we all share the same planetary home.

In the supernatural order of things our human solidarity is even more evident. We share the same guilt of original sin and the same Redeemer, who has raised us through grace to the status of beloved children of the heavenly Father. Again through grace, we form a close-knit mystical body in Christ. Therefore the first and overriding duty we owe this good Lord is to love him and, for his sake, our neighbour as well. "Every man," to quote Pope John XXIII's exhortatory words, "should feel in his heart the beat of his brother's heart."

Because nothing so effectively promotes charity as does prayer for our fellow-men, St. John Chrysostom observes, "Christ commands us to pray universally for the whole world." For that reason indeed he taught us the great prayer to the Father of All Mankind. It opens our minds and hearts to the dimensions of God's love and binds us together in the closest unity. Newman even saw the Our Father as a means of communing with all those who, since the time of Christ, have recited or will recite it.

Our filial prayer, then, is equally a brotherly one. It intercedes with our common Father on behalf of our brothers' concerns, interests and needs. And, in communing with our fellow-humans through prayer and charitable services, we anticipate here on earth our own eternal communion with the Three Persons communing with each other in the Godhead.

Bread for Our Neighbour

On a number of occasions the Christ of the gospel showed his concern and compassion for the hungry multitudes by miraculously multiplying loaves of bread and fish. Such importance does he in turn attach to our feeding the hungry according to our means that he made this a criterion upon which we will be judged at the end of the world. And the Judge will be none other than himself, mystically identified in this world with those who suffer hunger and thirst: "I was hungry and you gave me to eat. I was thirsty and you gave me to drink" (Mt 25: 35).

So it is with good reason that these two particular services feature among the so-called corporal works of mercy. And they further serve to explain why daily bread for our neighbour, not just for ourselves, merits a whole petition to itself in the Lord's Prayer. So let us reflect, each time we make this petition, that the merciful and loving God of providence does surely grant it by providing bread for some hungry mouths, though on this side of the grave we are most unlikely to know who exactly our beneficiaries are.

It is therefore imperative that, according to our circumstances, and in the measure of the possible, we not only pray for our hungry neighbours but supply them with food. St. James is very down-to-earth about this obligation. "Here is a brother, here is a sister," he says, "going naked, left without the means to secure their daily food. If one of you says to them, 'Go in peace, warm yourselves and take your fill,' without providing for their bodily needs, of what use is it?" (Jas 2: 15-16).

That great apostle of charity towards the poor, Frederic Ozanam, founder of the St. Vincent de Paul Society, instilled into it his own spirit of devoted service towards those lacking bread and other basic necessities. He regarded such service as our fulfilment of "a Christian law, a particular obligation of brotherhood." This obligation binding on Christians was well expressed by the Russian philosopher, Nicholas Berdyaev. "Care for the life of another, even material bodily care," he teaches, "is spiritual in essence. Bread for myself is a material concern, whereas bread for my neighbour is a spiritual one."

The Hungry Multitudes

Bread for my neighbour---this pressing concern takes on daunting and distressing proportions in today's world. For millions upon millions of our brothers and sisters in God are underfed and undernourished. Famine stalks many areas of the so-called Third World. Food-relief agencies cannot keep pace with the mounting total of hungry mouths and empty bellies in the various areas of urgent need. And we are only too sadly familiar with appeals made on their behalf---appeals displaying images of starving, pathetic human beings with protruding ribs, emaciated cheeks, matchstick limbs, and eyes that are hollow and pleading.

Most poignant and disturbing of all such pictures are those of helpless little children caught up in these grim starvation scenarios across the world. Elizabeth Browning's verse goes to the very heart of the matter:

> "Do you hear the children weeping,
> O my brothers?...
> The young, young children,
> O my brothers?
> They are weeping bitterly,
> They are weeping in the playtime of the others."

The Word Incarnate, who himself experienced hunger during his forty-day fast and miraculously fed a large multitude, feels a deep compassion for today's starving millions. But such is God's economy of salvation and providential plan that he relies on the cooperation of the favoured Western world to aid and feed, out of its own superabundance, the less fortunate members of the human race.

Let us here salute the various humanitarian agencies that are working so devotedly in the diffuse hunger-spots all over the globe. And let us continue to be as generous as possible in supporting their vital work according as our means allow.

Presently we shall be seeing what agricultural science and demography tell us about dealing with the food problems that cast such heavy shadows over the lives of millions. But first we need to dispose of a widespread myth concerning the ever-growing world population and the earth's capacity to feed the extra millions.

The Neo-Malthusian Myth

The myth in question takes its name from Malthus, who in the eighteenth century advanced the theory that we drastically need to curb the rise in world population because it necessarily outstrips the growth-rate in food supplies. Through failure to check population by prudential restraint, Malthus went on to warn, we are condemning future generations to a life blighted by food shortages if not actual starvation.

Today's neo-Malthusians make even more dire and alarmist prophecies, according to which our world will end up being hopelessly overcrowded and underfed unless we drastically reduce the population-growth. And the panacea they zealously propose and apply to this end in underdeveloped countries is artificial birth-control, sterilization, and abortion.

Besides being scientifically flawed and morally indefensible, neo-Malthusianism is a gross affront to the God of providence, the God whose wisdom and goodness are writ large across all creation. Besides, it implicitly rubbishes and invalidates the "daily bread" petition in the Lord's Prayer.

Blasphemy and Contraceptive Imperialism

Several eminent authorities in the field of agricultural science and demography have condemned neo-Malthusianism on grounds of poor economics. And its theology is poor as well. "When we try to restrict population growth artificially," wrote Dr Colin Clark, "we are not only making an economic mistake; we are blaspheming against divine providence." He and other experts, while accepting that we face a massive problem, maintain that it is one of food *distribution*, not production. They confidently estimate that, if maximxum use were made of all available resources and techniques, the earth could feed thirty billion people---that is, five times the present population. Moreover, it could do so at the high calorie level enjoyed by the average American family.

The same authorities point to the vast land areas throughout the world that are potentially arable and crop-productive if technical know-how and agricultural equipment were applied. Yet another reason for optimism is that a further source of highly nutritious food, with a potential overall yield at least equal to that of the earth, still remains almost entirely untapped: namely, the bed of the world's oceans.

A disturbing factor is that United Nations agencies are second to none in propagating the myth of global overpopulation, which they tie in with their promotion of "contraceptive imperialism," as it has been dubbed. Thus as a matter of policy their hand-outs are made conditional on the recipients' willingness to accept and implement their population-control agenda. A glaring example was to do with the relief offered to the Central American nations ravaged by Hurricane Mitch early in 1999.

War on Want

Our Father in Heaven is calling upon us in this third millennium to help fashion a world civilization that will be motivated by his love and based on his moral laws. And, furthermore, it must be a civilization enjoying an abundance of bread for all. In Pope John Paul II's words, "nobody must be excluded from the banquet of everyday consumerism." Here he is echoing Vatican II, which emphasized that the earth's bread, plus all the resources of material creation, are intended by the Creator for everybody; therefore it is his express will that these be justly and equitably distributed and shared.

The war on want is basically a war on underdevelopment. And it is imperative that we implement without delay a long-term policy for the countries concerned, a policy which can be summarized as helping people to help themselves. But in the meantime we must do all we can, and as quickly as we can, to deliver food and other essentials to stricken areas.

As was mentioned earlier, measures such as the maximum use of fertile land, proper methods of tillage, the arrest of soil erosion, the development of water supplies and irrigation schemes, the use of fertilizers, the application of modern farm machinery---agricultural techniques such as these have power to transform the bleakest of situations into one of prosperity and plenty.

Nor is it just the capacity to produce food that benefits by what Western scientific know-how has to offer. Improved food-production will naturally generate the development of industry and the raising of living standards. And these benefits will in turn spill over into areas such as education, health and general culture.

In urging us to do everything possible for our fellow-humans living in areas where food is scarce and poverty and illiteracy are rife, the Holy Father repeatedly underlines how hurtful this condition is to their dignity as human persons created in God's image and loved by him. He further exhorts us: "It is not only individuals who have opportunities to invite the poor to share in their prosperity. International institutions, national governments, and the centres controlling the world economy must all undertake brave plans and projects to ensure a more just sharing of the goods of the earth, both within individual countries and in relations between nations."

Cancelling Third World Debts

It is commonly acknowledged that John Paul II played a leading part in launching the initiative to wipe off all debts owed by Third World countries to various Western nations. He adopted the idea from ancient Israel's practice of cancelling all debts and freeing all slaves during jubilee years, which occurred every fifty years. And he went on to make his appeal for debt cancellation an integral part of his Jubilee 2000 programme.

Clearly, the cancellation, or at least the sizeable reduction, of debts is going to boost considerably the fragile economies of developing nations, also contributing thereby towards their food-producing capacity. And, by helping governments to finance educational and health programmes, the debt cancellations will likewise serve to reduce illiteracy and disease.

In fact, active steps have already been taken by several creditor nations to cancel, in large part if not entirely, the massive sums owed them by the so-called HIPC (Heavily Indebted Poor Countries). Divine providence will surely bless the creditor nations for their generous response to the appeal, a response which will happily in due course contribute substantially towards feeding the hungry, giving drink to the thirsty, and distributing fairly the good things and resources this world has to offer.

The Food that is Christ's Body

"Give us this day our supersubstantial bread" (Mt 6: 11) This rendering of the petition refers, in St. Jerome's judgment, to what he terms "our principal food." And by this he means the Eucharistic Christ, who frequently spoke of himself as the Bread of Life, the Living Bread who comes down from Heaven as nourishment for our spirits (cf. Jn 6: 35,48, 50). Christ's miraculous multiplication of loaves prefigured his far greater miracle of transsubstantiation---the changing of the substance of bread into the real, integral, enduring presence of the God-Man. This change takes place in the ritual known to the early Christians as "the breaking of bread" and to us as the Mass; that is, the sacramental re-enactment of the sacrifice offered by the Redeemer on Good Friday. An integral part of the Mass ritual is Holy Communion; we receive the Offerer and Victim as food for our souls, daily food to support us spiritually on our way to the heavenly homeland.

When St. Robert Southwell, the sixteenth-century poet-martyr, testified that "the God of hosts in slender Host doth dwell," he expressed a belief identical with that of the second-century martyr St. Justin: "The food which has been Eucharistized is the flesh and blood of the Incarnate Jesus." This is what we receive in Holy Communion, though in point of fact it is the sacramental God-Man who receives us, incorporating us deeper and deeper into his divine being and the inner life of the Trinity.

Another second-century martyr, St. Ignatius of Antioch, termed Holy Communion "the food of immortality." He did so in reference to the Lord's promise of resurrection to those who receive his Eucharistic body (cf. Jn 6: 54-56). This text tells us that the glorified Bread of Life is pledge of a risen and eternal existence for our body-soul selves. It also tells us, as do all the God-Man's words about the sacramental bread, how intensely he loves us---and longs for our return-love. Most appropriately, then, did St. Thomas liken the Eucharistic Bread to a divine hunger in search of our heart's hunger for God.

The Bread of God's Word

The petition for daily bread applies equally to another kind of hunger present in every human heart---the hunger for truth about ourselves, our Creator, and our destiny. What alone in this world can adequately satisfy this hunger is God's word. And for us Christians it comes principally through Scripture, the Church's teaching, and the liturgy. These various channels of God's word, we are assured by St. Augustine, constitute, just as much as does bodily food, "our daily bread, since they are necessities for our pilgrimage."

Our Lord himself referred to these necessities when, quoting the Old Testament, he said: "Not by bread alone does man live but by every word that proceeds from God's mouth" (Mt 4: 4). The Church in turn knows all about man's need for the bread that nourishes his spirit. For example, in one of its liturgical prayers it asks of the Father: "May your people find in your word the food of salvation and the fount of life."

Mother Teresa of Calcutta used to say that the poorest of the poor are not the materially deprived in the Third World but those multitudes in the so-called Fourth World---our affluent West---who are spiritually near-destitute and starving for lack of God's bread of truth and life. Though materially rich and highly developed, our Western world is spiritually a starveling in rags because it so neglects God and tramples on his laws.

Famine of the Spirit

The Russian philosopher, Alexander Solzhenitsyn, considered that the malaise underlying modern Western culture is that "people have forgotten God." Pius XII came to the same conclusion, lamenting that a soulless technology and mechanization have made modern man into "a giant of the physical world but have reduced him to pygmy proportions in the realm of the spiritual and the supernatural."

The saying of an Old Testament prophet aptly diagnoses the spiritual plight of the Fourth World; there prevails in it "a famine not of bread but of hearing the words of the Lord" (Amos 8: 11). In other words, the famine is of the spirit, affecting the minds and hearts of millions of our brothers and sisters, and reducing them to spiritual penury and wretchedness. For they lack the bread of truth and life so abundantly supplied by him who is the Eternal Truth and the Bread of Life.

We must therefore do all we can to bring them this bread. Moved by the urgency of the situation, Pope John Paul II issued, on the final World Mission Sunday of the century, a stirring call for all Christians to be missionaries of God's truth and love during the next millennium. What this requires of us above all, he underlined, is "a passion for the salvation of the world, and an ardent commitment to bring about the kingdom of the Father."

Chapter SEVEN

THE GOD WHO FORGIVES

In Graham Greene's novel, *Brighton Rock*, the central character---Pinkie---has for some years been caught up in a life of crime and sensuality. As a result, his conscience has become hardened and his attitude to life materialistic and cynical. Yet he can never entirely rid himself of a wistful nostalgia for his long-lost innocence and the consolations of the Catholic faith.

What mostly tugs at his memory is the Mass and everything associated with it---the flickering candles, the aura of sacred mystery, the atmosphere of holiness, purity and peace. As for the Agnus Dei---the sung invocation to the Eucharistic Christ---its melody often comes to haunt his waking moments, producing a stab of mingled remorse and longing when he finds himself rehearsing the words: "Lamb of God who takest away the sins of the world, have mercy on us. Lamb of God who takest away the sins of the world, grant us peace."

In the end the tormented Pinkie can no longer bear the inner anguish, the tug-of-war between past innocence and present turmoil. Overcome with despair, he finally leaps to his death from a high place into the ocean depths below.

Fact and Fiction

Pinkie's predicament and tragic end highlight in dramatic fashion something that is commonplace in present-day society. There are legions of real-life Pinkies around who know God and still half-want him, but feel hopelessly trapped in circumstances that violate his commandments and wound his love. In fact, theirs is the classic Prodigal Son situation. For their lives have become mired in broken commandments and guilt; the ache in their conscience can never be wholly sedated; and their Father's house seems to recede further and further out of reach with each day that passes.

Yet if these people could but realise that, as befits the Son of the all-merciful Father, the Lamb of God does indeed exercise the most tender mercy towards prodigals. And if only they could further realise how relatively easy it is for prodigals to return to the welcome ever awaiting them from their heavenly Father.

Before going any further, however, let us remind ourselves that, in a broad sense, all descendants of Adam and Eve are God's prodigal children, though some are more so than others. For at least in small ways everyone trespasses daily against the divine law and needs the Father's forgiveness.

We shall be returning to this theme presently. But first let us look at the mystery of sin as such; that is, how universal it is, what it is in itself, and what effects it produces with respect to God and ourselves. In consequence we shall be able to appreciate all the better how wonderfully forgiving is the Father of mankind, the Father of us trespassers, the Father whom a liturgical prayer acknowledges as "the God who reveals his almighty power chiefly in showing mercy and pity."

The Cry of the Beast

"There are two voices in man," the Curé d'Ars used to say, "the voice of the angel, and the voice of the beast. The voice of the angel is prayer. The voice of the beast is sin."

As nobody could reasonably deny, the beast-voice makes itself heard all too often in our own individual lives. With the sole exception of God's immaculate mother, who was preserved by special privilege from sinfulness of any kind, every human being transgresses God's law in various ways and to varying degrees. At least to this extent, then, each of us, let it be said again, is a prodigal needing to confess: "Father, I have sinned against Heaven and before thee, and am not worthy to be called thy child" (Lk 15: 18, 21).

That everyone is a sinner is also implicit in the fact that Our Lord instructed all and sundry to say: "Forgive us our trespasses." Hence every single person can fully identify with St. Peter when he prayed: "Depart from me, Lord, for I am a sinful man" (Lk 5: 8). Similarly we all have reason to make our own the publican's prayer: "Lord, have mercy on me, a sinner"(Lk 18: 13). Indeed, so blindingly obvious is our personal sinfulness that St. John bluntly brands anyone denying it a liar (cf. I Jn 2: 4).

The Saints and Sin

Everyone would agree that the following prayer by Newman is a model of sober realism, and we do well to make it our own. Humbly and truthfully he asks: "What is my life, dear Lord, but one series of offences, little and great, against thee?" Let us note that not even the greatest saints are exempt from this category. They too must humbly recite their Confiteor for breaches, howsoever minor, against the divine holiness. Thus the Book of Proverbs significantly affirms that even the just may stumble into sinfulness as many as seven times a day, though they rise from that state immediately (cf. Prov 24: 16).

So it is that from every human self there rises the voice of the beast, the cry of sin, muted though it is when coming from God's holy ones. However, like all mortals they no less must duly ask the Father to pardon their trespasses, howsoever light and slight they may be.

Interestingly enough, a celebrated mystic, St. Catherine of Genoa, was once prompted by humility to make the following request of God: would he allow her to see, as he did, the true state of her soul? Her prayer was granted. She found herself enveloped in a bright light that revealed several blemishes caused by imperfections on her part. So horrified was she by this spectacle, and unable to endure it a moment longer, she begged God to take away that all-revealing light immediately.

The Sins of the World

Because sin is a reality deeply engrained into the very texture of human lives, it is also and inevitably woven closely into universal history. So much so, that a distinguished historian, Professor Herbert Butterfield, commented: "What history does is to uncover man's universal sin." This verdict was endorsed by another authority, Lord Acton; he confessed to feeling appalled at the sheer amount of sin and evil buried away in the annals of the past.

To revert to the Curé d'Ars' metaphor, the cry of the beast coming from so many untold millions of human beings across the centuries swells to a deafening roar, a monstrous chorus of guilt and shame. Take the millennium to which we so recently bade farewell. While being in so many respects rich in human achievements, it was steeped in sinfulness of every kind, not least during its closing twentieth century. Besides witnessing two horrendous world wars, which sprang from the politics of envy, greed and hatred, it also saw the rise and fall of two evil empires---Communism and German National Socialism---which openly denied God, rejected the commandmments, and committed crimes against humanity on an unimaginable scale.

But even the combined moral evils associated with these two tyrannies have been eclipsed and out-horrored in our day by an even more savage tyranny---a tyranny which has witnessed, and continues to witness, the wholesale butchery of multitudes of pre-born infants at the hands of abortionists.

Massacre of the Innocents

What this means is that a latter-day massacre of the innocents is taking place all over the globe on a scale that dwarfs all the atrocities committed under Communism and Nazism combined.

A conservative estimate currently puts the annual world-wide total of aborted infants at tens of millions. Which amounts to saying that anything up to one billion defenceless little human persons were not allowed to see the light of twentieth-century day. And the carnage continues unabated. Without any doubt this is the sin of sins that cries loudest of all to Heaven for vengeance.

In his document preparing us for the third millennium, Pope John Paul II had the abortion issue prominently in mind when he lamented that many people today have lost "the sense of sin." Besides stressing the need for conversion and the renunciation of past sinfulness, he encouraged us to promote in every possible way what is good and holy in public life. And this should include whatever support and cooperation we can offer, not least the prayer of reparation, towards stemming the tide of sinfulness in general, and of the ever-expanding evil of abortion in particular.

Other moral evils besides stained the past century. Suffice it to say that there has been a growing neglect of God and flouting of his commandments. Add to that the results of what has been called "the sexual revolution," which is much aided and abetted by more accessible and effective methods of birth control.

The Originating Sin

Catholic theology tells us that all human trespasses flow from the first-ever trespass committed by our First Parents, Adam and Eve, at the dawn of mankind's history. Original sin we call it, and it arose at the instigation of the devil. It is passed on to us with and through the transmission of human nature.

Though original sin is not personal to Adam and Eve's posterity, we nevertheless contract its guilt as well as its penal effects; which effects include an imbalance within ourselves between reason and instincts and a resultant propensity towards sin. Scripture refers to it as "the down-dragging tendency to sin which so easily besets us" (Heb 12: 1).

So every sin we commit is as it were fall-out from that originating offence against God's law. Again, every sin we commit is, like its prototype, fundamentally due to wilful pride and self-love at the expense of humility and the love of God. Which state of affairs prompted Shakespeare to speak of "the offending Adam" within our primogenitor's multitudinous offspring.

Again to quote Graham Greene, the sin of Adam and Eve was "the original calamity by which the world has been overcrowded with lust and crime and unhappy love." More serious still, the world was deprived through original sin of God's grace---the indispensable means of attaining eternal life. But the all-merciful God intervened redemptively and with superabundant generosity in fallen man's favour. St. Leo the Great hailed this stupendous gift as follows: "Christ's inexpressible grace gave us blessings better than those the devil's envy had taken away."

The ABC of Sin

Having seen something of sin's reality and universal outreach, we must now briefly look at sin in itself; that is, what it is and what it does. St. Anselm provides us with a handy and helpful formula. "Sin," he teaches, "is nothing else than man's failure to render God his due."

A big advantage of this formula is that it appropriately reflects St. Matthew's version of the Our Father, in which he refers to sins as so many debts we owe God. This was in fact the Jewish perception of sin; namely, an evil for which we require pardon from the divine Lawgiver as from a spiritual Creditor. Accordingly, the debt we owe our fatherly Creditor is genuine sorrow for our transgressions backed up by our readiness to render due satisfaction for them.

The common definition of sin is that it is an offence against the commandments of God or of the Church, by thought, word, deed or omission. Sin's bottom line is that it involves on our part what St. Thomas terms a turning away from God and a corresponding turning towards some illicit temporal satisfaction.

Serious breaches of God's law are termed mortal sins because they break off relations with God and extinguish his grace-life within us. Venial sins, on the other hand, while not rupturing that vital relationship with God which brings us his life-giving grace, offend him nonetheless and can easily dispose us towards falling into serious sin. The term venial denotes that such transgressions are more easily forgiven than mortal ones.

A useful metaphor was suggested by Frank Sheed to illustrate the respective effects of mortal and venial sins. Think of the human soul, he says, as an electric bulb. When in a state of grace, it is radiant with light. But if the filament is destroyed, the light is extinguished; so too is the light of grace snuffed out by mortal sin. If, on the other hand, the bulb is merely dusty and smudged, the light will still be there, though obscured and diminished. Herein we see an image of venial sin's effects on the human soul.

A Sense of Sin

The fatherly Creditor against whose law we trespass readily remits our debt of guilt and punishment when we ask his forgiveness. St. Ignatius recommends that we should further ask him for what he calls "a sense of sin." By this he means a vivid and realistic awareness of sin's evil and malice, which will clearly help us to avoid offending God even by the most insignificant of peccadillos.

In order to gain the desired perspective on sin, St. Ignatius further counsels us to look at it in the light of God's immense majesty, grandeur and glory. Never forget, the saint points out, that the Lord against whom we dare trespass is no less than the Almighty Creator, the all-holy Author of the moral law, our sovereign Master and Ruler. By defying his will and violating his commandments we wantonly set ourselves up in opposition to the great God of Heaven and earth. Like Lucifer and his fellow-rebels we reject the Almighty's dominion over us as the Source of our being and abandon him as our Ultimate Goal. A further factor is that the malice of our transgressions, even the most trivial, itself takes on quasi-infinite proportions inasmuch as it offends the Infinite Being.

Sin is therefore heinous and abominable, and has appropriately been compared with a malignant cancer within the human spirit. Sin is mutiny against our bountiful, all-holy Father, the Master of our destiny. And, as several mystics have been specially enlightened to behold, sin defaces and dishonours God's divine beauty reflected in us, his images and likenesses.

Through their closeness to God the saints develop an acute awareness both of his holiness and our human sinfulness. St. John Chrysostom used to say that the only thing he feared in this world was sin. And Queen Blanche, mother of St. Louis, King of France, spoke words to him as a boy which were to shape his whole future life. "Much though I love you," she told him, "I would prefer to see you dead rather than committing one single mortal sin."

For mortal sin offends God so gravely that it becomes the graveyard of his grace in the soul. In St. Augustine's words: "The body dies when the soul departs; but the soul dies when God departs." St. Thomas put it more strongly. "The body of an impenitent sinner," he says, "is a tomb covering a soul dead by sin." And St. John Vianney put it strongest of all, likening a soul in mortal sin to a rotting carcase being dragged through the streets.

Making the Angels Weep

It would be impossible to exaggerate the weight of the moral debt mankind owes God---a debt to which each and all have contributed. In fact, every generation needs a prophet to indict its moral depravity as Esdras did his own: "O my God," he prayed, "I am all confusion. I am ashamed to lift my eyes towards thee, so deep, head-deep, are we sunk in the flood of our wrongdoing, so high, Heaven-high, mounts the tale of our transgressions. Sinful fathers begot us; sinners are we to this day. Ours is the fault; we stand before thee guilty, and without excuse" (1 Esdras 9:6-7, 15).

Corresponding to their distinctive brand of defiance against God, our transgressions assume a variety of forms. It was their range and scale that Shakespeare had in mind when he wrote:

> "Man, proud man...
> Plays such fantastic tricks before high Heaven
> As make the angels weep."

These words serve to remind us that "we present a spectacle to the whole creation, men and angels alike" (I Cor 4: 9). It is comforting to recall that God's angels, our appointed guardians in particular, watch over us with loving care, ever solicitous to keep our feet from straying into the paths of sin. And the God of angels himself has testified that they rejoice over any sinner repenting his wrongdoings (cf. Lk 15: 10).

Sin and Christ's Sufferings

It is important to realise that sin, far from being merely a transgression against an abstract commandment, has a profoundly personal dimension. For it directly offends no less than the three Divine Persons, the Second of whom expiated mankind's total wrongdoings through his bitter sufferings and death.

The saints are sensitively aware of the connection between our sins and the Passion of Christ. St. Francis of Assisi, for instance, addresses these words to us all: "Nor did demons crucify him. It is you who have crucified him and crucify him still, when you delight in your vices and sins." Some spiritual authorities have even correllated specific types of sin with the different kinds of suffering inflicted on the Saviour. Thus St. Augustine saw man's evil thoughts as being quasi-instrumental in the crowning with thorns. And St. Teresa of Avila was not alone in linking sins of the flesh with the scourging at the pillar.

The Roman Catechism similarly emphasized the connection between man's transgressions and the corresponding agonies of the Passion. "Sinners," it says, "were the authors and ministers of all the sufferings that the Divine Redeemer endured." The text continues: "Since our sins made the Lord Jesus suffer the torments of the cross, those who plunge themselves into disorders and crimes crucify the Son of God anew in their hearts and hold him up to contempt. And when we deny him by our deeds, we in some way seem to lay violent hands on him."

An identical message is found in the Church's modern Catechism. There we read: "It is precisely in the Passion, when the mercy of Christ is about to vanquish sin, that sin most clearly manifests its violence and its many forms: unbelief, murderous hatred, shunning and mockery by the leaders and the people, Pilate's cowardice and the cruelty of the soldiers, Judas' betrayal, Peter's denial and the disciples' flight."

He Loves to Pardon

Because it is God against whom we trespass, it is his prerogative to pardon. And pardon us he does. In fact, "he loves to pardon," as an Old Testament prophet reassures us. Warming to his theme, he continues: "Was there ever such a God, so ready to forgive sins, to overlook faults?...He will relent and have mercy on us, quashing our guilt, burying our sins away sea-deep" (Michaeas 7: 18-19).

As one would expect, the New Testament is even more reassuring about divine mercy. And we have only to look at a crucifix to see why. How tremendously forgiving God is was well understood by St. Catherine of Siena. "He is more ready to pardon," she declared, "than we are to sin." Many instances are recorded in the gospels of the God-Man exercising his pardoning power---and never more movingly than when, hanging on the cross, he pleaded with the Father on behalf of his executioners: "Forgive them, for they know not what they do" (Lk 23: 34).

The crucified Saviour's merciful words apply to sinners generally. For we break God's commandments without fully comprehending what we do; that is, without a clear idea of how unthinkably evil and malicious sin is in itself. In saying which we run into a strange irony: namely, it is precisely sin---both original and personal---that seriously weakens our capacity to grasp its true significance. Not that this excuses us entirely from the resultant guilt. But awareness of our weakened understanding of sin's evil should encourage us (as we saw earlier) to ask God to increase our sense of sin lest we become cavalier and careless about offending the Most High.

The Divine Mercy

> "There's a wideness in God's mercy
> Like the wideness of the sea."

This verse from a well-known hymn conveys the essence of the devotion known as the Divine Mercy. Based on the revelations made by Our Lord to Blessed Faustina Kowalska, it was officially approved by the Holy See in 1978. In these revelations Our Lord presents himself as the Fount of the Father's Mercy, claiming such titles as Jesus Mercy and Mercy Incarnate. Hereby he is reminding us that the redemptive mission given him by the Father makes him a refuge and shelter for sinful humanity---its most sinful members in particular. Furthermore, he links the Divine Mercy devotion with faith and trust in his true presence in the Eucharist. For there, in person, substantially and really, we find him, the God-Man, the Father's Mercy Incarnate, the all-loving Holy One, the all-forgiving Mighty and Immortal One.

Through this fresh and appealing devotion, which has rapidly achieved a world-wide resonance, Our Lord is highlighting his immense mercy and readiness to forgive. Especially to those who feel themselves entrapped, enmeshed in sin, he offers his all-merciful Self as a lifeline, an anchor of salvation. He well knows that the present-day world more than deserves the indictment levelled by St. Paul against his own generation---a generation he described as mired in "fornication, impurity, licentiousness, sorcery, enmity, strife, jealousy, anger, selfishness, dissension, factions, envy, drunkenness, carousing, and the like" (Gal 5: 19-21).

The Lord of Divine Mercy instructed Blessed Faustina to make the following entry in her diary; it sums up the whole purpose of his mission to our fallen selves. "I have opened my heart as a living fountain of mercy. Let all souls draw life from it. Let no one fear to draw near to me, even though their sins be as scarlet. My mercy is greater than your sins and those of the entire world. I allowed my Sacred Heart to be pierced by a lance, thus opening wide the source of mercy for you. Come, then, with trust to draw graces from this fountain. I never reject a contrite heart."

The Sacrament of Mercy

What we also find in Blessed Faustina's diary is a reference by Our Lord to the sacrament he instituted precisely in order to bring his pardoning mercy to sinners; it is variously referred to as Confession, Reconciliation, Penance. The diary entry in question reads: "Write, speak of my mercy. Tell souls where they are to look for solace---the tribunal of mercy. There the greatest miracles take place and are incessantly repeated. It suffices to come to the feet of my representative and reveal one's misery to him, and the miracle of divine mercy will be fully demonstrated."

The gospels testify that Christ not only claimed for himself the divine prerogative to forgive sins (cf. Mt 9: 2-7) but also commissioned and empowered his priestly ministers to forgive sins in his name(cf. Mt 18: 18).

However, the sacrament's ministration is by no means limited to the priest's role. The recipient too is required to make his contribution to the sacramental dynamics. It is a threefold contribution. First of these is contrition---perfect if it arises from love, imperfect if from fear. The second contribution is the penitent's avowal of guilt, while the third is satisfaction, namely, his willingness to accept and perform whatever penance is imposed by the priest in reparation for the sins confessed.

What, then, are the formal effects of this sacrament? In the first place, it reconciles the sinner with God if serious unconfessed sin(s) featured in his avowal of guilt, besides restoring him to a state of grace. A second effect of the sacrament is the remission of the eternal punishment due on serious and unrepented sin. In addition, confession remits, at least in part, the temporal punishment attaching to all sins.

God's Charity and Tenderness

So much for the formal or objective effects of God's sacrament of mercy. Its subjective, that is, psychological, effects are also considerable. By banishing the feeling of guilt, Confession produces in penitents---particularly those with mortal sin(s) on their conscience---a deep sense of release and relief. At the same time it revives their self-respect and self-confidence, buoys up morale, reinforces resolution, and builds up sin-resistance. The Council of Trent specifically names among the sacrament's benefits "inward peace and serenity of conscience," adding that these are commonly accompanied by "overpowering spiritual consolation."

No wonder, then, that God's great sacrament of mercy has been so highly praised by many eminent thinkers---including non-Catholics and also non-Christians---as an institution which, even considered at a purely human level, combines deep psychological wisdom and compassion with a huge amount of good, sound commonsense. Pascal says of Confession: "Can anything be thought of more charitable or more tender?" Newman's bouquet is also worth quoting. "If there is a heavenly idea in the Catholic Church," he reasoned, "then surely, next after the Blessed Sacrament, it is Confession."

No wonder either that frequent Confession (even if only venial sins need to be confessed) is warmly recommended by so many saints and by every single Pope from St. Pius X onwards. Pius XII championed the practice with particular zeal. "By frequent Confession," he urged the universal Church, "we grow in a true knowledge of ourselves and in Christian humility; bad habits are uprooted; spiritual negligence and apathy are prevented; the conscience is purified and the will strengthened; salutary spiritual direction is obtained; and grace is increased by the efficacy of the sacrament."

In commending frequent Confession, John Paul II describes it as "the sacrament where God's mercy meets man's misery." He further observes: "The personal encounter with the forgiving Jesus is a divine means which keeps alive in our hearts and in our communities a consciousness of sin's perennial reality and tragedy, and increases our holiness."

The Father of Purgatory

The penalties due on our sins are also remitted by God our Father through what we might call the auxiliary agencies of Purgatory and indulgences. Purgatory is that zone where departed human spirits (we know them as the holy souls) undergo penal sufferings on account of their sins---sufferings that are also purifying and thus prepare Purgatory's inmates for admission to the Beatific Vision.

To be sure, the guilt attaching to the sins committed by the holy souls has been forgiven; but whatever penance may remain outstanding on those sins must at all costs still be rendered to divine justice. Which explains Purgatory's whole point and purpose. Through its purifying pains, sinful but forgiven souls pay the Divine Creditor whatever moral debts of expiation and satisfaction may still be owing on account of their trespasses.

The doctrine of Purgatory introduces us to that profound and consoling reality known as the Communion of Saints. This stands for the vital bond of unity and fellowship between all members of Christ's mystical body, be they in Heaven, on earth, or in Purgatory. Accordingly we can forge links of love and prayer with our brothers and sisters on both sides of the grave.

The Father of Indulgences

As for the souls in Purgatory, we are also able to bring them relief and solace through our prayers and suffrages. Moreover, we can thereby not only reduce their debt of expiation but even cancel it out altogether. That is to say, we can win for them the equivalent of a total amnesty, thus liberating them instantly from their penitential prison into the welcoming embrace of the heavenly Father.

Here we are dealing with what are technically known as indulgences---a further indication of how compassionate the Father is with regard to sin's penal consequences. Indulgences are simply let-offs from the purgatorial penance owing to divine justice; a partial indulgence remits a portion of a soul's sentence, while a plenary indulgence remits it entirely and instantly.

What makes indulgences possible is the so-called treasury of the Church. This comprises, to begin with, the infinite merits of Christ, added to which are the merits of the Blessed Virgin as well as all the martyrs and saints. Together their merits create an inexhaustible common treasure-chest, from which the Church draws when declaring and administering indulgences.

"The Eucharistic sacrifice is the best way of bringing relief to the dead." St. John Chrysostom is here voicing a conviction about indulgences that goes back to earliest times. And nobody appreciated its significance better than St. Monica; she specially asked her son---St. Augustine---to remember her at the altar. The Father of mercies is surely pleased to see us in turn exercising, through our prayers and the indulgences we apply to others, a maximum of mercy towards the holy souls in their prison of pain and purification.

Purgatory Manifests Sin's Evil

A further indication of sin's intrinsic evil and how offensive it is to Almighty God can be discerned in the degree of expiation it demands in purgatory. On this subject, the very last man to overstate or exaggerate anything---St. Thomas---affirms that the minutest particle of purgatorial pain is more severe than the heaviest imaginable sufferings on earth. He even goes on to say that what the holy souls have to endure is severer than anything Our Lord suffered during his bitter Passion. Similarly the seventeenth-century Carmelite, St. Mary Magdalen of Pazzi, drawing on her mystical experiences with regard to Purgatory, stated that words failed her in describing its torments. In comparison with them, she would only say, "the dungeons of the martyrs are gardens of delight."

As We Forgive Others

The Lord's Prayer makes one thing very clear: the Father's forgiveness of our trespasses hinges upon our willingness to forgive those who trespass against us. Our human forgiveness is therefore the vital prerequisite, the indispensable condition, for us to receive divine forgiveness.

St. Augustine taught this lesson in a very down-to-earth way. "If you are suffering from an evil man's injustice," he counsels, "forgive him---lest there be two bad men!" In other words, by withholding forgiveness towards others we not only forfeit God's pardon for our own sins but add an additional one to their tally---a sin against the virtue of charity, which, among its multiple operations, forgives injuries and offences.

In this respect Our Lord set a supreme example, even forgiving those who were nailing him to the cross (cf. Lk 23: 34). He also gave us an admonitory lesson in his parable about the debtor who, having just been mercifully absolved of a heavy debt, proved harshly unforgiving towards someone owing him a good deal less (cf. Mt 18: 23-35).

Forgiveness of others, Christ insists, is a duty binding on his followers. Indeed, reconciliation with our fellow-men must even precede any gift-offering we make to God (cf. Mt 5: 23-24). And our forgiveness should, if necessary, be exercised seventy times seven and beyond (cf. Mt 18: 21-22). "If you will not forgive others," Jesus says elsewhere in words that mirror the Lord's Prayer petition, "neither will your Father in Heaven forgive you your sins" (Mk 11: 26).

The importance of forgiveness in the Christian programme is often underlined by St. Paul. "Be kind to others," he teaches, "and be mutually merciful and forgiving, even as God has forgiven you in Christ" (Eph 4: 32). Another text reads: "Bear with one another and forgive one another, if any have a complaint. Even as the Lord has forgiven you, so do you likewise" (Col 3: 13).

In Forgiving You are Forgiven

However, as many of us have discovered for ourselves, forgiving others their trespasses can prove to be easier said than done. Amid the inevitable stresses and strains arising within human relations, people can, and all too often do, trespass against each other in minor or major ways. Here the scope is endless. Injuries and offences, hurts and harms, can range from the tremendous to the trivial. St. Augustine illustrates this by comparing a man's irritation at someone's immoderate laughter and his reaction if an enemy were to burn his house down.

But, whatever our neighbour's offences and injuries, the Lord's imperative remains iron-clad: we must forgive them from our heart if we would expect like treatment from God. "Blessed are the merciful for they shall obtain mercy" (Mt 5: 7). Shakespeare's couplet expresses this same principle:

> "Who from crimes would pardoned be,
> In mercy should set others free."

But setting others free, let it be repeated, is easier said than done. For we cannot anaesthetize our instinctive hurt and anger when others injure and offend us. What does lie in our power, however, is mercy and pardon. "The heart that offers itself to the Holy Spirit," the Catholic Catechism reminds us encouragingly, "turns injury into compassion and purifies the memory by transforming the hurt into intercession."

"Intercession"---therein lies the magic formula. By praying for those who hurt us or harm us we not only benefit them but alchemize our bitterness and worse into forgiving love and peace. Hard though it may be to apply, the intercession formula works---and can work wonders. For it harnesses the mighty resources of gospel charity, which not only gives and forgives but heals and consoles the giver and forgiver. Chesterton's saying sums it all up: "Charity means pardoning what is unpardonable or it is no virtue at all."

A Sermon To Remember

Finally, it was a theological genius and saint---Gregory of Nyssa---who left us an amazing and memorable exhortation on the vital link between divine and human forgiveness. Taken from one of his sermons, the exhortation evokes the uninhibited boldness and even audacity of a child full of confidence in its loving Father. "In the Lord's Prayer," the saint told his congregation, "Jesus wants your forgiving disposition to be a good example to God! For we invite him to imitate us, since we equivalently say: 'Do thou the same as I have done, Lord. Imitate thy servant, though he be only a poor beggar while thou art the King of the Universe. Lord, I have shown great mercy to my neighbour; do thou now imitate thy servant's charity!'"

Chapter EIGHT

THE GOD WHO DELIVERS US

In declaring the year 2000 a Jubilee Year, the Pope stressed that its underlying point and purpose was to celebrate the 2000th birthday of Jesus, Son of the Virgin Mary. As for the underlying point and purpose of his coming into our world in the first place, it is enshrined in the very name given him from the beginning: Jesus, which means Saviour, Deliverer.

Yes, Jesus is the Son of God sent by the Father to save us, that is, *to deliver us from evil*---a phrase he himself would later incorporate into the Lord's Prayer. What, we may ask, was the evil in question? As will be shown, it takes a variety of forms. But common to them all is that they owe their origin to one single agent---the devil. For it was at his instigation that evil of every kind entered God's creation. St. John says explicitly: "The reason why the Son of God appeared was to destroy the works of the devil" (Jn 8: 44).

So it is that, each time we recite the Lord's Prayer, we are literally asking the Father to deliver us from the devil's baleful handiwork, the main manifestations of which we'll be looking at presently. Needless to say, Satan has by no means withdrawn from the human scene after making his first and highly successful foray into it at the dawn of history. On the contrary, he remains incessantly and restlessly active down the ages, sparing nobody as he seeks to spread his kingdom of evil far and wide.

In other words, the devil's handiwork is an ongoing operation. St. Paul's phrase indicates how keenly aware he was of this: "The mystery of evil is ever at work" (2 Thess 2: 7). And in numerous other instances Scripture alerts us to the ever-present menace posed to the world at large---and to each of us individually--- by God's enemy and ours, the instigator and architect of all that is evil in the moral and material order alike.

The Rise of Evil

Because Satan is such a key player in the cosmic drama, we clearly need to know something about who and what he is. Originally called Lucifer and endowed with superlative gifts, he was one of God's supreme archangels. But, alas, motivated by pride and disobedience, he became a commanding figure in the angelic revolt against the known will of their Creator. In consequence he and his fellow-renegades became demons, wilfully bringing down upon themselves the evil of separation---radical, irrevocable separation---from God, in whom alone can his rational creatures, whether angelic or human, find their true happiness and fulfilment.

Thereupon, as we read in the Genesis account, the fallen Lucifer, filled with envy and spite towards our first parents, destined as they were for that eternal beatitude which he himself had rejected, successfully seduced them from their obedience to the Creator. That is, he induced them to commit the first-ever human offence against God's commandments; we know it as original sin.

Original Sin's Evil Consequences

Now such was the status of our protoparents in that moral probation that they represented all mankind; that is to say, they stood proxy for their posterity, namely, the entire human race. Consequently each single one of us inherits the guilt of their sin. What they further bequeathed to their descendants were the penalties resultant upon their transgression, the most disastrous of which was the loss of sanctifying grace and, therewith, the eternal happiness to which it alone gives access.

Likewise forfeited for themselves and for us were three priceless privileges that had been conferred by the Creator upon our primogenitors. The first of these gave them perfect control over their body-soul selves, thus eliminating anything like disharmony or conflict between reason and animal instincts. Once deprived of this control, however, they were subject to concupiscence, which is an inclination, a propensity, to break God's commandments. An inspired author terms it "the down-dragging tendency to sin which so easily besets us" (Heb 12: 1).

The second privilege terminated by original sin was the overall well-being of the material order. Hereby is meant that physical evils such as sickness and suffering had no place in God's original plan for mankind. The same applied to bodily death, immunity from which was the third privilege forfeited by the originating couple for themselves and all humanity.

As for the fourth evil, which had already come into being as punishment for the sin of the angels, and which now in turn poses a deadly threat to everyone descended from Adam and Eve, it is the mystery of Hell. This is the state of eternal damnation, the infernal abode, which Lucifer and his fellow-rebels arrogantly and defiantly chose rather than submit to the divine will.

Fall-Out from the Fall

As many theologians have commonly pointed out with regard to original sin, we'll never fully comprehend just how gravely evil it was in itself and how ruinous were its effects on man himself, on his earthly environment, and on his eternal destiny in particular. Though of all revealed truths original sin is in many ways the most incomprehensible, yet without it, as Pascal shrewdly observed, we human beings would be utterly incomprehensible to ourselves.

The bottom line of that first-ever human sin is that, like Humpty Dumpty, its perpetrators and all their descendants had a great fall---a calamitous fall from God-given treasures such as grace and original justice, immunity from the evils of concupiscence, sin, pain and death, and, worst of all, from the prospect of eternal happiness in the glory of God. To sum things up, all this and Heaven too became casualties of that primordial and ruinous transgression.

Man's moral fall has been likened to a sin-explosion, the severe penal consequences of which constitute the equivalent of fall-out. And because each of these consequences is in its own way the deprivation of a positive good intended by our Creator, they are rightly called evil. We have no choice, of course, but to accept them as just punishment not only for original sin but for our own personal sins. However, thanks to God's redeeming grace we can do much to reduce and mitigate the effects of these various evils. More importantly, we can use them as precious means for drawing closer to God.

So, with the faith that seeks understanding, let us now consider the main manifestations of evil brought into our world, including our personal world, through the envy of the fallen Lucifer.

As we have been seeing, these evils are fivefold. We begin with our morally-weakened and sin-inclined condition due to concupiscence and temptations, from which proceed our sins and guilt. Next we'll treat of the evil of pain and suffering, to be followed by the still worse evil of bodily death. Our fifth and final consideration will be that mystery which out-evils all others: the reality and threat of eternal damnation, and Satan's raging zeal to lead us there.

The Unholy Trinity

> "Where is one that, born of woman,
> Altogether can escape
> From the lower world within him,
> Moods of tiger and of ape?"

Thus did Tennyson describe in poetic and graphic form the tug-of-war that goes on in every conscience between good and evil, between what St. Paul calls our higher self and our lower self, the flesh and the spirit. Temptations coming from the flesh are the illicit urges and drives resulting from concupiscence, which is an inner disequilibrium leading us in the direction of the seven capital sins. St. James says of concupiscence that "it draws a man away by the lure of his own passions" (Jam 1: 14). And St. Augustine, referring to his unregenerate days, related that concupiscence "put him on a rack between flesh and spirit."

But concupiscence, which Scripture commonly speaks of as "the flesh," is not alone in bringing temptations our way. The world and the devil too play their part. Together this threesome make up what has been nicknamed "the unholy trinity." In this context "world" is better referred to as "worldliness," since it connotes the false maxims and unprincipled attitudes that can so insidiously draw our hearts away from loyalty to God and his service. In addition, worldliness tempts us through the attractiveness of bad example and the psychological pressure to conform. Another thing about worldliness is that it is far more concerned with political correctness than with moral rectitude.

The third of the unholy trio we have to contend with is the devil. With great skill and untiring industry he endeavours to insinuate sinful images into our imaginations and stir memories of past sinfulness, his purpose being to lead us into forbidden desires and actions. He encourages every form of avarice and selfishness, aiming throughout to entice us into sins of pride and thence to other offences. His ultimate aim, of course, is to bring us eventually into his own kingdom of damnation without end.

Lead Us Not into Temptation

The traditional wording of this clause in the Our Father is apt to be misleading, inasmuch as it appears to contradict a principle laid down by Scripture. St. James, for instance, states categorically that "God cannot be tempted by evil and he himself tempts no one"

(James 1: 13).

As it happens, the French version of the Lord's Prayer comes nearest to what this phrase is really saying; that is, it asks the Father "not to allow us to yield to temptation." This chimes in with another rendering that was popular in the early Church: "Father, do not suffer us to be led into temptation exceeding our strength."

Whatever phraseology is adopted, however, it is clear that God's whole concern is to set us free from evil, not lead us into it. The Catholic Catechism, clearly influenced by the French wording of the Lord's Prayer, offers this commentary: "We ask God not to allow us to take the way that leads to sin." On identical lines was the prayer written by St. Augustine. "Father," he pleads, "reach out thy hand to me. Hold thy light before me and recall me from my strayings, so that with thee as my guide I may return to myself and to thee."

Life is One Continuous Temptation

The prophet Job voiced an indisputable truth when he wrote: "Is not man's life on earth one continuous temptation?" (Job 7: 1). We all know only too well from experience that temptations and trials are part and parcel of existence in this world; indeed, so integral are they to the human condition that we can scarcely conceive of life without them.

Moreover, to seek divine aid for our innate weakness against temptation is perhaps the most instinctive and spontaneous of all the petitions in the Lord's Prayer. For it springs from our awareness of the dangers posed jointly by our fallen human nature, this fallen world, and malicious fallen angels.

On the positive side, many authors remind us that temptation and trials can play a useful and upbuilding role in our lives, helping us know ourselves and our evil inclinations better, besides encouraging us to place ever-greater trust in God. St. Paul wrote: "I pray that no temptation may come upon you that is beyond man's strength. Not that God will play you false; he will not allow you to be tempted beyond your powers. With the temptation itself, he will ordain the issue of it, and enable you to hold your own" (I Cor 10:13).

Helps Against Temptation

One of St. Philip Neri's favourite prayers was: "Lord, do not trust Philip!" This echoes the Pauline caution: "Let he who stands take heed lest he fall" (I Cor 10: 12). And the Lord himself has reminded us that the spirit is willing but the flesh is weak (cf. Mt 26: 41).

What we learn herefrom is that over-confidence in our own resources can prove disastrous. The same applies to the neglect of prayer; indeed, the Saviour who encountered the Tempter in the desert has pointedly instructed us to watch and pray lest we enter into temptation (cf. Mt 26: 41). Another thing to beware of is a lack of vigilance; this calls for continuous custody of the senses, prompt resistance to temptations, especially at their initial stage, and avoidance of the occasions of sin.

Regarding the last-named, Benjamin Franklin offered this sensible counsel: "Keep thee from the occasion," he said, "and God will keep thee from the sin." We are also warned against flirting with potential danger and "playing with hellfire," as moral risk-taking has been called. Pascal made this observation on the subject: "We run carelessly to the precipice after having put something before our eyes to prevent us from seeing it!"

St. Teresa of Avila is most helpful and practical about how to proceed in the spiritual battle. "Strive to walk with love and fear," she advises. "Love will make you quicken your steps. Fear will make you look where you are setting your feet so that you may not fall." And if we do happen to fall, she further exhorts us, we should not grow discouraged and lose heart, since this can lead to despair and eventual eternal loss. Rather, we should straightaway say sorry to the Lord, pick ourselves up, and re-enter the fray, fuller than ever with confidence in the strength that comes from God.

The Evil of Sin

The preceding chapter has already explained what sin is and does, besides dealing with God's great mercy and forgiveness. Hence it suffices here to recall that sin, resulting as it does from temptation and human weakness, gives rise to that aching evil which is a guilty conscience. God's forgiving love delivers us from this, and likewise delivers us from those other evils we bring upon ourselves through serious sin: namely, the loss of sanctifying grace and the menace of eternal damnation.

When, therefore, we ask the heavenly Father to deliver us from evil, we implicitly include our sinfulness in general and, in particular, any actual sins on our conscience. Hand in hand with this petition should go our resolve to make frequent acts of contrition and to resort regularly to sacramental reconciliation.

The Evil of Suffering

Atheists like Nietzsche have accused Christians of worshipping suffering. But this is utterly false. What we do worship is a Sufferer---the Man of Sorrows whose redemptive sufferings and death transformed that historic Friday two millennia ago into Good Friday. And it is so called because it marked the beginning of our deliverance from the evils due to original sin, one of which, we don't need to be reminded, is suffering of mind and body.

We shall return to the redemptive value of the Saviour's sufferings. But let us first focus on our own so as to get a broad picture of the realities involved. Our sufferings take two forms---spiritual and bodily; herein they are equivalently the Gethsemanes and Calvaries that can and do enter our lives so unexpectedly and uninvitedly.

Spiritual suffering lodges in our thoughts, desires and memories, and at its worst is agonising and intense. G.M. Hopkins' lines capture something of the anguish it produces:

> "The mind has mountains,
> Cliffs of fall frightful,
> Sheer, no-man-fathomed."

Spiritual suffering comes in a whole variety of forms. We think here of states of mind such as sadness and depression, loneliness, separation from loved ones, bereavements, failures, disappointments, snubs, humiliations, frustration, worry, anxiety, fear and uncertainty, the feeling of being unloved and unwanted, the torment of an unquiet conscience.

Bodily sufferings are equally protean and come in all shapes and sizes. Thus they can be trivial or tremendous, passing or permanent, merely inconveniencing or totally incapacitating. They can vary from headaches to hernia, pinpricks to paralysis, blindness to cancer. They range from mere scratches and bruises to the hideous injuries and disfigurements that can result from road accidents. And they can strike at anyone, anywhere, and at any time. Dylan Thomas was altogether realistic in speaking of "the everywhere of grief."

What Do We Ask For?

In this petition we are certainly not asking our heavenly Father to deliver us entirely from suffering and sorrow. For these evils, being an inescapable inheritance from the original sinners themselves, are now integral to and inseparable from our earthly existence. They are the hard facts of life in a fallen world. A character in Shakespeare makes this reflection on our human situation:

> "Comfort's in Heaven, and we are on the earth,
> Where nothing lives but crosses, care and grief."

What we *do* ask of our heavenly Father is that He will take away, or at least mitigate, any suffering, sickness, worry, fear, etc, that is overshadowing our lives here and now. That is, whatever chalice of bodily or mental pain life may put to our lips, we should, like our Master in the Gethsamane garden, ask the Father to take it away---if this pleases his holy will (cf. Mt 26: 39). St. Bernadette's counsel is pure gold: "In any physical or mental pain, we must say only 'Yes, my God,' without any ifs, without any buts."

What we are also implicitly asking the Father in this petition is to deliver us from any doubt about his good and wise purposes in allowing us to suffer. He is, after all, "a gentle Father and the God of all consolation" (2 Cor I: 3). St. Augustine says of him: "Because he is supremely good, he would never allow any evil whatsoever to exist in his works if he were not so powerful and good as to cause good to emerge from evil itself."

What, then, is the good that God extracts from the evils of suffering and sorrow? First of all, it is our humble and ready acceptance of the divine will, together with complete trust in his providential love. Secondly, it is our sanctification through being obedient to God, as St. Francis of Assisi attested in his prayer: "Blessed be you, Lord, for our Sister Suffering, which we can divinize by our union with you, and which in return sanctifies us." A third good to emerge from the evil of suffering is our configuration to the Christ of the Passion.

Christ's Co-Sufferers and Co-Workers

The suffering and the sick are Christ's living and transparent images. And no one grasped this reality more clearly than Mother Teresa of Calcutta. "O beloved sick," she wrote, "how doubly dear you are to me. You personify Christ, and what a privilege is mine to be allowed to tend you."

It was his discovery of this mystical identity between the Divine Sufferer and every human being laden with a cross that inspired Claudel to say: "Jesus did not come to explain away suffering or to remove it, but to fill it with his presence. " And the same discovery led Oscar Wilde to declare: "Suffering is not a mystery but a revelation."

What is further revealed through suffering is its power, when united with Christ's, to merit grace for the sanctification and salvation of souls. Pope Paul VI saw deeply into this mystery. Addressing the world's sick and suffering at the end of Vatican Two, he said: "You are the aristocrats of the kingdom of God. And if you but choose to do so, you work out with him the world's salvation."

The significance of this is that sufferers, by filling up what is wanting in the sufferings of Christ for his body, the Church (cf. Col 1: 24), become cooperators in those sufferings and thus share in his redemptive work---as did his Mother to a supreme degree. Further, we know how she taught and encouraged the little Fatima seers to offer sacrifices along with prayers for souls dying in mortal sin. We also know how victim-souls, moved powerfully by God's grace, make it their whole vocation, their special apostolate, to offer their sufferings in expiation for the sins of the world and for the salvation of sinners. The German mystic, Blessed Anna Schaeffer, called her sickroom "a workshop of suffering." And Teresa Neumann remarked cheerfully from her bed of pain: "As most of my time is taken up with suffering for souls, this has become my profession."

The Evil of Death

If our first parents had not sinned, ours would be a world without undertakers, graves, cemeteries and crematoria. For death, which entered the scene through the devil's envy, was a direct consequence of original sin (cf. Wisd 2: 23-24) in that God withdrew the preternatural privilege of bodily immortality.

The first thing to be noted about death is that it is integral to our human being. Biologists inform us that the millions of cells comprising our bodies must inevitably suffer total breakdown. Which means that death necessarily ensues when the body can no longer respond to the life-giving energies of its informing vital principle---the human spirit. Accordingly man is mortal because bodily death is inescapable, inexorably so. This sombre truth finds memorable expression in Shakespeare's sonnet: "Golden lads and girls all must, as chimney-sweepers, come to dust."

For this reason, then, death is very much an evil, and we must accept it and its pains for what they are: punishment for the ancestral guilt handed down from our first parents, as well as for our personal sins. And because death is in itself such a grim and unpleasant reality, it is understandable that pagans ancient and modern regard it with a mixture of sorrow, horror, despair, and occasional helpless rage, for it is "the dying of the light."

The Redemption of Death

But for us Christians the perspective on death is altogether different. Our Master's redemptive sacrifice of his life has stripped death of its former sting and victory (cf. I Cor 15: 55). Which it did by opening up the prospect of the body's glorious resurrection into a paradisal world beyond.

Hence St. Francis of Assisi could joyously exclaim: "Blessed art thou, O Sister Death, who art for me the gate of life." And we can all say with St. Paul: "To live is Christ, and to die is gain" (Phil 1: 21). Lacordaire even exhorts us to look forward to our deathday as "the most beautiful day of our lives." And, as did the early martyrs buried in the Roman catacombs, we should celebrate that day as our *dies natalis*, our birthday into the glorious new world God has ready for those who leave this present one in his peace and friendship.

Preparing for Death

One of the evil aspects of death is the uncertainty of its when, its where and its how. And this obviously calls for constant vigilance on our part. Indeed, Our Lord frequently drew our attention to this need, comparing death to a thief who will break in when least expected. "Be on the watch, then; the day of it and the hour of it are unknown to you" (Mt 25: 13). Similarly, in one of its litanies the Church asks God to deliver us from "a sudden and unprovided death."

With good reason, then, traditional Christian piety encourages us to pray for a "happy death." This connotes, above all, that we are in a state of grace when that all-decisive moment arrives; it further connotes those additional graces we stand to receive should we happen to benefit by the sacraments of the dying. Altogether so important, indeed momentous, will be the hour of our death that, each time we recite the Hail Mary, we ask the Mother of God in advance to assist us with her presence and her prayers.

Benedictine monks are recommended in their founder's Rule "to keep death daily before their eyes," while St. Ignatius enjoined all members of the Society of Jesus to glorify God in their death *even more* than in their lives. For he recognized that the act of dying is the ultimate meritorious act we shall be able to offer God; therefore we are to make of it a masterpiece.

Deliver Us from the Evil One

Last but certainly not least, it is from our enemy the devil and his threat of damnation that we ask to be delivered in every Our Father we say. In fact, the word for "evil" in the Greek text of the prayer stands equally for "evil one." Hereby, of course, is meant the former angelic star and supremo who committed the first-ever offence against the divine will and, in so doing, became Satan, the implacable enemy of God as well as of God's human images.

What, then, is the devil's overriding desire and purpose in our regard? It is to make like shipwreck of our eternal destiny, thus committing us forever to what Scripture calls "Satan's prison" (Apoc 20: 3, 7), and which Christ spoke of as "the everlasting fire prepared for the devil and his angels" (Mt 25: 41). The Evil One's paramount activity is well expressed in the lines:

> "He kindles on the coast false fires
> That others may be lost."

As Pius XII is on record as saying, divine revelation has its "frightening aspects," and the prospect of final impenitence and everlasting punishment is one of them *par excellence*. Nevertheless, eternal damnation in Hell, unthinkable though it may be, cannot by any means, *pace* many liberal theologians, be dismissed as a mythological horror story or some barbarous Gothic fantasy rooted in primitive fundamentalism. Rather, it is a dogmatic truth and therefore not to be doubted, still less denied. The Athanasian Creed, for example, affirms: "Those who have done evil will go into eternal fire." And the Dogmatic Constitution of Benedict XII states: "The souls of those who die in personal grievous sin descend immediately into Hell, where they will be tormented by its pains."

Of these pains the most bitter is the so-called pain of loss. It means that, as do the demons, damned souls suffer the agony of being deprived for ever of the vision and possession of God. Hell's secondary punishment is called the pain of sense; it consists in the infliction of positive punishment through an external agency going under the name of fire, which, albeit of the physical order, is unlike any earthly fire. However, we are allowed to believe that hellfire can be understood in a purely metaphorical sense; that is, as symbolizing spiritual pains, notably the torments of conscience.

The Teaching of Christ

Hell's grim reality was uncompromisingly taught by Christ himself. Repeatedly in the gospel he warns unrepentant sinners of the divine retribution awaiting them in the fire of Gehenna, adding that in the infernal abode "the worm that eats them never dies, the fire is never extinguished" (Mt 9: 44).

In addition, many of Our Lord's parables end with the condemnation of the wicked to Hell. And he likened our journey through this world to one of two roads leading respectively to an eternity of life or perdition. On another occasion he enjoined us to "fear him who can destroy both body and soul in Hell" (Mt 10: 28).

But surely the most impressive of gospel warnings is found in the terrible malediction due to be pronounced on the reprobate by the Christ of Judgment Day: "Depart from me, you cursed, into the everlasting fire!" (Mt 25: 41). In the face of all this evidence, denial of Hell's reality is therefore tantamount to denying not only the gospel of Christ but, in the same breath, the Christ whose gospel it is.

The Second Death

St. John described damnation in hell as "the second death in the lake of fire" (Apoc 20: 4). As distinct from the first or biological death, this second or eschatological death denotes the perpetual separation of a human being from its Creator, the Infinite Being who alone can fill that abyss which is the human heart.

We gain many fresh insights into the City of the Second Death from the testimony of those mystics whom God has allowed to glimpse something of its horrors. To give some examples. St. Teresa of Avila was so affected by her vision of Hell that, even after an interval of six years, she still felt "chilled with fear at the very thought of it." And in a lapidary phrase she summed up her impressions of hell---its furious fires, its cruel demons, its animalised humans, and its cacophany of curses and blasphemies---as "a place without God." St. Lydwine was shown the interior of Hell by her guardian angel. But she could not bear the sight of the flames and the torments. Still less could she endure the shouts of rage and despair mixed with blasphemies. St. Frances of Rome reacted in much the same way. Subsequently the very mention of Hell would fill her with horror at the memory of "its gehennal flames, the animal-like figures, and the unholy bedlam of blasphemy and hate."

Then there is the testimony of the young Fatima visionaries. One of them, Lucia, became a Carmelite nun, and wrote, at her bishop's request, an account of what they had experienced in 1917: "We saw as it were a sea of fire. Plunged into it were demons and souls in human form, amid shrieks and groans of despair, which horrified us and made us tremble with fear. It must have been this sight which caused me to cry out, as people say who heard me."

Fearing God---and Hell

Karl Rahner has pointed out that an underlying value of the doctrine of Hell is to instil the fear of God into us and so bring us to our senses. He further explains: "The dogma of Hell means that human life is threatened by the real possibility of shipwreck, because man freely disposes of himself and can therefore freely refuse to give himself to God."

St. Benedict specifically recommends his monks to keep constantly alive within themselves "the dread of Hell." As for St. Thomas More, he frequently asked God for the grace "to foresee and consider the everlasting fires of Hell." And many a saint has done the same, including Ignatius, Francis Xavier, Francis Borgia, Teresa of Avila, and the Curé d'Ars. The last-named coined a useful maxim with regard to this practice. "He who really fears Hell," he said, "will not fall into it."

The Two Cities

St. Paul viewed all human history as a battlefield where God's followers are locked in combat with the powers of darkness led by the fallen Lucifer (cf. Eph 6: 12). This Pauline vision gave rise to St. Augustine's concept of the Two Cities, each of which solicits for its own ends the spiritual allegiance of mankind: the City of God and the City of Satan. Depending on whether or not he is in a state of grace at any given moment, every individual is a citizen of one or the other. St. Ignatius in turn developed this spiritual polarisation of the human race into what he termed the Two Kingdoms---Christ's and Satan's---perpetually at war within human souls and for their winning.

Yes, it is immortal souls that are at stake in the deadly ongoing clash between good and evil. Padre Pio saw this issue with the utmost clarity. "The field of battle between God and Satan," he stated, "is the human soul. It is there that the battle rages every moment of our lives." The battle in question is waged over the two eternities---one of life with God, the other that ultimate horror which is the second death. Hence the constant need for vigilance on our part. St. Bernard has said the last word on the subject: "No security is too great when eternity is at stake."

What is starkly highlighted by this non-stop spiritual warfare is the value of human souls. Each is an immortal diamond, having been created by God in his image so as to enjoy forever a shining destiny in his kingdom of life and love. But each man must merit this destiny for himself by submitting his created freedom to the will of his Almighty Creator. Moreover, he must continue to do so all the way through life's journey up to his final breath---that fateful moment when his soul reaches the crossroads between time and eternity. St. Francis of Sales offers us guidance that is both wise and practical: "We are walking in this world between Paradise and Hell, and our last step will place us in an everlasting dwelling."

Deliver All of Us

Finally, the word "us," as in all the petitions of the Lord's Prayer, serves here to remind us that we belong to one big human family under the Fatherhood of God. Accordingly, we pray that, besides ourselves, all our brothers and sisters the world over will be delivered from evil in general, and from the monumental evil of eternal loss in particular. A glowing example for us to imitate in this matter was provided by the three Fatima seers; acting on Our Lady's instructions, they regularly offered prayers and sacrifices for dying sinners, especially those who had no one to pray for them.

God 2000

Chapter NINE

MOTHER OF GOD 2000

The only fairy story that is true, claimed Chesterton, is the one that took place in the Bethlehem stable on Christmas night. Certainly the stock ingredients of fairy stories as such are amply verified in its scenario. To begin with, there's an innocent and beautiful heroine---Mary, the princess of grace and now a proud and radiant young mother. Then there's her new-born Son lying in the manger, stealing the show and winning all hearts as infants do; though still tiny and helpless, he is the Prince of Peace, the Lord of Lords, and the Desire of the Eternal Hills. Finally, there's the heroic, watchful figure of St. Joseph standing protectively in the background

Meanwhile the Bethlehem hills are alive with the sound of music as the angelic hosts carol the new-born King. Meanwhile, too, and not to be left out of any fairy tale worthy of the name, there lurks an ogre breathing out threats and destruction. This one's name is Herod, and already he is plotting to shatter the lovely but fragile idyll set in the Bethlehem stable. In the end, however, and again in true fairy-story style, the monstrous tyrant is foiled when St. Joseph, alerted to the peril by an angel, leads his precious charges to safety.

Thank You, Father, for Emmanuel

This all-too-true fairy story lies at the heart of our Christian faith and takes on a very special resonance at this present time. For we are celebrating the birth of Jesus two millennia ago, the birth which has made such a mighty impact on subsequent history.

Our celebrations are further meant to renew and fortify our belief in Christianity's central mystery---the Incarnation. We understand hereby the gracious coming into our world in human form of the Father's co-equal, co-eternal Son. Thus the Father's Word became the Word-made-flesh. Now and forever he is Emmanuel, the God-Man dwelling among us, a divine Person vested with a nature as human as our own. Thus he can do such things as behold us through human eyes, breathe our air, share our joys and sorrows, suffer bitter bodily pains for our redemption, and love us deeply with a heart of flesh.

All this and more is wrapped up in the stupendous gift our heavenly Father made us on Christmas night, and we thank him for it from the bottom of our hearts.

Thank you, Father, for Mary

We further thank the Father for creating, sanctifying and preparing the woman who made all this possible. We mean, of course, Mary, whose praises, as she herself predicted, have been sung by her devotees in every successive generation. But of the millionfold bouquets God's mother has received, few can be more gracious and courtly than the one offered by St. Anselm of Canterbury; he hailed her as "wonderfully singular and singularly wonderful...beautiful to behold, lovely to contemplate, delightful to serve."

Mary's whole secret is that she was a key instrument in the Father's plan to salvage human destiny from the wreckage of original sin. This wholly sinless daughter of Israel was called to be leading lady in the drama of Jesus, the drama of human redemption and salvation. St. Francis of Sales rightly styles her "the vital link between God's greatness and human wretchedness."

Like Mother, Like Son

The Blessed Virgin's role in the divine plan was and remains pivotal. For in the first instance she gave her free and full consent to be the God-Man's mother, thereby "setting in motion the salvation of the world," to quote St. Irenaeus.

It is amazing to reflect that, because Christ's conception in Mary's womb was a virginal one, in genetic terms his human heredity was therefore drawn exclusively from the primary maternal cell supplied by his mother. That is to say, from her alone he derived those multiple somatic and psychosomatic factors which ordinarily are the combined genetic contribution of both father and mother.

From this it can be deduced that her Son's humanity was totally Marian. In other words, Christ the Man is in Mary's image and likeness; in more senses than one he is his mother's Son. Doubtless his contemporaries would immediately have recognized this in his facial features, his temperament, his emotions, the accent and tonality of his voice, his gestures and mannerisms, his smile, and in many other ways besides.

Nor was Our Lady's role limited to conceiving her Messianic Son and bringing him into the world; she brought him up in this world as well. In St. Augustine's memorable words, "Mary gave milk to our Bread," later teaching him to lisp his first baby words, toddle his first faltering steps, recite his first prayers. In a word, she was at his side and service all the way from those tender early years till the bitter end in Good Friday's noonday darkness.

It is only right and fitting, therefore, that we should also pay a special honour to the mother of God 2000 as we celebrate his Incarnation in her womb those many years ago. For the entire divine plan hinged directly upon her saying Yes to the proposal brought by the Archangel Gabriel. And, thank God, say Yes she did. In Rahner's words, "Mary's voice became the voice of all mankind."

Mary's New Relationships

What Our Lady's consent likewise brought about was her exalted new relationship to the three Divine Persons. For she was now and forever the most favoured daughter of the Father, mother of the Son, and spouse of the Holy Spirit. What equally took on an exalted new status was the mother of God's relationship to mankind at large. For in his dying moments her crucified Son personally appointed her spiritual mother of all those for whom he was enduring this agony, namely, the descendants of Adam and Eve.

As is unfailingly the case with any appointment coming from God, an accompanying grace commensurate with the duties and needs involved was granted to the mother of mankind. What, then, is the precise function of this unique grace, this mega-grace, conferred upon Mary? The answer is that it enables, empowers, inspires her to mother-love, in God and for God, the entire human race. She is thus its universal mother. In saying which we are not simply being rhetorical or giving Mary a title that is nothing above honorific. Rather, her universal motherhood literally means that she loves mankind as the family entrusted to her by her Son.

Mary Mother-Loves Each Individual Person

Yet this does not imply that only in a collective or general way does Mary's mother-love embrace the human race spread around the globe. On the contrary, and wonderful to recall, her love focuses at the same time, personally and tenderly, upon each and every one of the six billion persons currently comprising the world-wide totality. Indeed, so divinely pure and ardent is this maternal love burning in Mary's immaculate heart for each and all that we can claim, as did St. Aelred: "She is even more our mother than our natural mother." Pius XII endorsed this consoling truth in his encyclical on Christ's mystical body, stating that Mary bestows on all individuals "that same motherly care and fervent love with which she fostered the suckling infant Jesus in the cradle."

A clear indication of how our heavenly mother's universal love co-exists with her personal love for every member of her world-wide family is found in the symbolism of the Miraculous

Medal, where she is depicted with her feet resting on a globe. She herself explained its meaning to St. Catherine Labouré: "This globe represents both the whole world and every single soul."

Mother of Divine Grace

Pope John Paul II has hailed the Virgin Mary as "the morning star of the new millennium." As mankind's mother as well as God's, she surely has special graces in store for her universal family now launched into yet another millennium to flow calendar-wise from that far-off Bethlehem event. But before considering what these graces are likely to be, a helpful preliminary will be to survey Our Lady's role in the distribution of this precious commodity.

Yes, grace is by far the most precious commodity we can possess in this world, since it is a sharing in the very life of the three Divine Persons. For this reason it is equivalently God's gold, the currency of his kingdom on earth. If only we could appreciate this heavenly treasure for what it is! Shakespeare's lines speak for us all: "O mortal grace of mortal man that we more hunt for than the grace of God!"

Co-Redeeming with and under Christ

Now Mary's essential gift, as the angel of the Annunciation attested, is that she possesses this divine life in its fullness. And in consideration of her maternal role and functions, she bears the title Mother of Divine Grace. Her general role, as we have seen, is to be mother of the Redeemer and the redeemed alike. As for the functions belonging to this role, they are threefold.

In the first place, as the Redeemer's mother Mary collaborated with him to the full in his lifework and deathwork alike. In so doing she became, to the most marvellous degree, what every Christian is called to be: namely, a co-worker or coredeemer with the sole Redeemer in a secondary and subsidiary capacity (cf. 1 Cor 3: 9). But so intimate and unique was Mary's collaborative contribution to her Son's redemptive work, especially when she offered him to the Father on Calvary along with her own bitter anguish, that she is recognized as the coredeemer *par excellence*. Indeed, to mark this distinction she has duly been designated the Coredemptrix. This, then, is the Blessed Virgin's first role in the economy of grace, a role that has long been acknowledged in traditional Catholic doctrine and devotion centred on Mary as the New Eve.

Mediatrix and Advocate

The second function of the Mother of Divine Grace is consistent with her role as the New Eve mother-loving her world-wide family. As mothers do, she feeds and nourishes her children. And the food and drink she supplies---that is, mediates---is the supernatural life of grace.

Moreover, Mary's mediation applies to every single grace we receive; hence her further title Mediatrix of All Graces. Again we are dealing with a truth enshrined in traditional belief and devotion going back to earliest times. It was to find popular expression in St. Bernard's saying: "God willed us to have all through Mary." Which Hopkins subsequently clothed in poetic dress: "She mothers every grace that does now reach our race."

Mary's third function as Mother of Divine Grace is as the Queen-Mother ever-present before the throne of God, where she unceasingly intercedes on our behalf for the graces we need. On this account she is titled our Advocate. As John Paul II has said of God's Queen-Mother: "She is the spokeswoman of her Son's will, knowing she can point out to him the needs of mankind." The title Advocate similarly embodies a truth rooted in age-long Catholic belief and devotion.

Marian Light for our New Millennium

"The morning star of the new millennium," to quote the Holy Father again, surely wishes to mark the occasion by blessing the human race entrusted to her maternal care with the special graces it needs. As was noted earlier, her love focuses on every individual on earth, not failing, however, to take cognizance of the various nations---all of them so different---to which the individuals belong.

This is reflected in the mother of God's recently---acquired title as Our Lady of All Nations. In its official icon she is portrayed, as is the case with the Miraculous Medal, standing upon a globe. Additionally, however, a flock of sheep is depicted below the globe. Their significance, the Mother of God explained to Ida Peerdeman, the Amsterdam visionary, is that they symbolize mankind's various races and peoples, all of which together form the flock belonging to Christ, the Good Shepherd.

What Lessons Can Mary Give?

Now God knows, and so does his mother, our world badly needs the light and strength of his grace as it forges ahead into the opening century of the new millennium. But what particular lessons, the question naturally arises, does the Mother of God have to offer us?

A long list of deserving suggestions could be put forward. However, we are spared the trouble of assessing them, because, as a matter of fact, the major lessons needed by our world are precisely those we have been considering in the Lord's Prayer. This being a perfect summary of the gospel message, its petitions accurately reflect, as in a mirror, the principal guidelines given by the God-Man for humanity to achieve holiness and wellbeing in this world and salvation in the next.

Because God's immaculate mother virtually personified the high ideals of the Lord's Prayer, we therefore stand to gain much further illumination from her glowing example. So let us revisit the Our Father petitions, reviewing them this time from what might be called a Marian perspective. As we shall see, the exercise will deepen our understanding of the gospel values involved, besides helping to improve our shabby performance in their regard.

By going through the Lord's Prayer with Mary, we shall fully realise that she truly is what Paul VI said of her: "The first and most perfect of Christ's disciples." In addition, the former star pupil in the school of Christ is now a leading teacher, the Seat of Wisdom herself. She has abundant guidance and encouragement to offer not only Christian believers but all men and women of good will.

Mary Hallows God's Name

Hailed in the early Church as the Panhagia---the All-Holy---God's mother achieved the high ideal towards which Christ wants all to aspire. "Be ye perfect," he enjoined us, "as your heavenly Father is perfect" (Mt 5: 48). Her consummate perfection prompted Newman to remark: "Can we set bounds to the holiness of her who is the mother of the Holiest?"

In this petition Mary reminds us that our prime duty as the Father's creatures is to hallow or sanctify his name, that is, to offer him praise, reverence, homage, service; and, in the process, to become hallowed ourselves. Mary excelled in this programme, as her joyous hymn of praise and thanksgiving (we know it as the Magnificat) testifies. Pope John Paul II names Mary's inspiring masterpiece her "spiritual testament," further pointing out how well it matches the prayerful and joyous nature of our Jubilee celebrations.

Mary's example as the perfect hallower teaches us, above all, the value of prayer. It must become the breath of our lives so that they in turn become, like hers, a lived Magnificat. It is along these lines that we are exhorted by St. Ambrose: "In each one of us may the soul of Mary praise the Lord, and may the spirit of Mary exult in God." Incidentally, prayer before the Blessed Sacrament offers particularly rich scope for us to unite ourselves with God's perfect hallower, Our Lady of the Magnificat, in offering the Eucharistic Emmanuel adoration, praise and thanksgiving.

Mary and God's Kingdom

It is a leading idea among the Fathers of the Church that Mary's initial great act of faith and acceptance of her mission plays a major part in the conception of Christian believers as God's children, thereby gaining them access to his kingdom. This identical thought underlies Paul VI's teaching on the subject. "The mother of God," he writes, "the New Eve, the Mother of the Church, carries on in Heaven her maternal role with regard to the members of Christ, cooperating in the birth and development of divine life in the souls of the redeemed."

No one has ever said "Thy kingdom come" with greater faith and fervour than did the mother of God. With regard to the inward aspect of that kingdom, which makes us temples of the Trinity, she reached a degree of union with the indwelling Lord unsurpassed by any other creature. Which gave rise to the saying: "Mary shines among the saints like the sun among the stars."

One of this inward kingdom's vital elements is the virtue of faith. Herein, too, Mary excelled beyond all others, not only believing more strongly but reaching a profound understanding of faith's mysteries. We must therefore ask her frequently to obtain for us a faith that is strong and enlightened. Another major help provided by Mary concerns the kingdom's external manifestation- the Church. She will lead us to cherish it with deep love and loyalty, its human failings notwithstanding. To the Church's magisterium or teaching office we owe absolute obedience, accepting its doctrines with submission of both mind and heart.

Regarding specifically Marian doctrines, Paul VI drew our attention to an additional value attaching to their proper understanding: they provide us with what he calls "a key to the exact understanding of the mysteries of Christ and the Church." For, as the old adage affirms, "Mary alone destroys all heresies." In other words, a right understanding of Marian truths unerringly exposes falsehoods and worse in other doctrines.

A particular virtue greatly prized by Our Lady is zeal for the spread of God's kingdom. To possess this is to share in the love Mary and her divine Son have for priceless human souls and their eternal salvation. Three of Mary's titles proclaim her consuming zeal for the souls redeemed by her Son: Mother of the Church, Queen of Apostles, and Star of Evangelizaton.

Thy Will be Done

"God's will," St. Paul teaches, "is our sanctification" (1 Thess 4: 3). As it happens, the reverse is equally true: our sanctification consists primarily in obeying the Father's will. Our Lord himself made this clear on several recorded occasions in the gospel. As for his mother, she made compliance with the divine will the guiding principle of her life; thus she remained the handmaid of the Lord all the way from her Yes at Nazareth to the dark hours on Golgotha.

Mary's obedience to the will of God was total and impeccable. So there was a delicious and intended irony in her Son's remark that only those merit to be called his mother, his sisters and his brothers who do his Father's will (cf. Mt 12: 50; Mk 3: 35). A further imperative of Christian discipleship is obedience to the Church's teachings and ordinances. For to heed the Church is to heed its Founder (cf. Lk 10: 16). In this and in all respects it is both wise and sensible to follow Our Lady's counsel at Cana: "Do whatever He tells you" (Jn 2: 5).

A great lover and servant of Mary was St. Maximilian Kolbe; he founded the so-called Militia of the Immaculate, the members of which consecrate themselves to the mother of God and put themselves under her close guidance, realising that she, more than anyone else, can lead us to "the unsearchable riches of Christ" (Eph 3: 8). "We wish," the saint wrote, "to do the will of the Immaculate One, to be perfect instruments in her hands, to be totally guided by her, in perfect obedience."

Mary and Our Daily Bread

We saw earlier that, in biblical usage, bread can stand not only for all foodstuffs but for everything we need for our daily lives. So in asking the Father to give us our daily bread, we are in effect asking him to provide us with all our various requirements. Now to see the part Mary can and does play on our behalf in this petition.

"Mary is music in our need." Newman's dictum acknowledges Mary's providential role in supplying us with what we need. Chaucer does the same, addressing God's mother as "treasurer of bounty to mankind." This fits in with her mediatorial role; which means that as Mediatrix she acts as the channel of all God's mercies to mankind. Thus Jacinta, the little Fatima seer, was instructed during an apparition to announce that "all graces come to us through the Immaculate Heart of Mary."

We know from the gospel how frequently Our Lord encouraged us to make the prayer of petition. And the Cana episode provides an instance when his mother succesfully petitioned him on behalf of a bridal couple. The consoling truth is that as our Advocate she presents our every petition to God. And she does so all the more effectively when we specifically ask her to intercede for the favours in question. So powerful and effective is Mary's intercessory power that she has been called "suppliant omnipotence." Newman supplies a classic text on this subject. "Her office above," he explains, "is one of perpetual intercession for the faithful militant. More than all the angels and saints she has this great prevailing gift of prayer. No one has access to the Almighty as his mother has; none has merit such as hers. Her Son will deny her nothing that she asks; and herein lies her power."

Our Need for Bread

In an earlier chapter we considered the three main applications of the word "bread" as it appears in the Our Father: namely our material needs; the word of God, since man does not live by bread alone (cf. Mt 4; 4); and the Eucharist. Let us see how in each of these areas our gracious Advocate comes to our aid.

As the Mother of Mercy she must view with infinite compassion the starving millions in today's world. And we for our part should daily and specifically ask her to bless the efforts of all who endeavour to feed those many hungry mouths. Also we should ask her to hasten the day when the victims of famine can be enabled to solve the problem for themselves.

Regarding the spiritual food that is the word of God, it is a dire necessity for great multitudes of people, not least those living in the so-called Fourth World---our affluent West with its state-of-the-art technology co-existing with spiritual near-destitution. The people affected by which, let us ever recall, are each and all sons and daughters of the Queen of Prophets, the mother of God's Eternal Word.

Thirdly there is the Bread of Life, the Living Bread that comes down from Heaven for the life of the world. A beautiful truth is expressed in the words of an ancient Ethiopian liturgical prayer. "Glory be to Mary," it says, "who brought us the Eucharist." Having brought us this priceless gift, the mother of the Eucharistic Jesus now yearns for him to be brought into as many lives as possible and as often as possible. If we can help at all in this direction, she will reward us as only she knows how.

The Refuge of Sinners

"All except the mother of God must truly say, 'Forgive us our trespasses.'" Thus did the Council of Carthage affirm Mary's lifelong sinlessnes---the fruit of her exemption from original sin. Thanks to these privileges, the Blessed Virgin is a living flame of holiness, the personification of Christian perfection. "She is all light," the young Fatima seers reported of Mary, while Francis Thompson spoke of her "white immaculacy."

Yet, paradoxically, the sinless mother of God is the Refuge of Sinners, the Virgin Most Merciful, the Mother of Mercy---to cite three of her official titles, all of which were greatly cherished by the Curé d'Ars. "The heart of this good mother," he said of her, "is all love and mercy. The greater the sinner, the greater is her tenderness and compassion." Mary has also been called "the guardian of the treasures of God's mercy." For, as mother of Jesus Mercy as well as of us, she both supplicates and mediates his forgiving grace to her contrite children.

"Contrite"---this is a key word in our dealings with God, since it opens for us the gate of his forgiveness. Many saints have made the expression of sorrow for sin their favourite ejaculation. St. Francis Xavier, for example, constantly repeated, "Jesus, Son of David, have mercy on me." Indeed, he died with these words on his lips.

Confession and Purgatory

We see why Our Lady so emphasizes, as she did at Lourdes and Fatima for example, the importance of contrition and reparation for sin, also recommending frequent recourse to the sacrament of forgiveness. For its specific and merciful graces, she knows best of all, include a strengthening of our resolution to avoid sin in the future.

What our heavenly mother also knows best of all is how intrinsically evil sin is in itself and in its effects. Besides offending the infinite Creator, it was instrumental in inflicting such grievous wounds upon the humanity he assumed for our redemption. Our merciful mother will surely obtain for us if we ask her that choice grace which is so much needed in the contemporary world; St. Ignatius named it "a sense of sin."

Where, we may wonder, is to be found the last outpost of divine mercy? Its name is Purgatory, where human souls are purified while they pay God the debt of expiatory suffering still due on past forgiven offences. As several saints and mystics have testified, Mary, the merciful Queen of Purgatory, urges us to be generous in offering prayers and gaining indulgences for her children suffering in that twilight world midway between Heaven and earth, a world where God's justice and mercy meet and kiss.

Deliverance from Evil

Being the chosen handmaid of the Father who delivers us from evil, Our Lady participates most closely in this merciful work. Here we shall focus on the help provided by her in those three areas of evil that cast such heavy shadows over human lives: namely, sufferings and sorrows; the prospect of death; and the threat of eternal damnation posed by the fallen angels.

Sufferings and Sorrows

Each time we recite the *Hail, Holy Queen* prayer we remind the mother of God, if this were necessary, that our world is not only a place of exile but a valley of tears. She knows it all too well from her own bitter experience. Her future role as the Mother of Sorrows was prophetically proclaimed by the aged Simeon: a sword of anguish would transfix her soul on account of her Messianic Son. And transfix her soul it did with a vengeance during the dark hours of the Passion.

When sorrows come our way, let us confidently ask our heavenly mother to remove them or at least bring us ease and comfort. But, as she did, we must submit ourselves entirely and lovingly to what God our Father wills. Similarly with bodily sicknesses and sufferings; let us invoke Our Lady's help---but always with that same proviso: God's will, not our own, must prevail.

It is reassuring to recall that our loving mother's eyes of mercy notice every single cross, little or great, that life happens to place on our shoulders. And unfailingly through her intercession comes the grace enabling us to carry our crosses lovingly and cheerfully. It is further reassuring to recall that sufferings and sorrows accepted in union with her Son's and offered co-redemptively with them become transmuted into the gold of grace for the benefit and salvation of precious souls.

The Hour of our Death

Next to consider that evil which is bodily death. A measure of its key importance in our lives can be seen in the fact that in every Hail Mary we ask our holy mother to pray for us at that fateful crossroads between this world and the next, between time and eternity. Hence the need on our part for vigilance and preparedness---as Christ emphasised in the gospel (cf. Mt 25: 13).

Newman says comfortingly on this subject: "If Mary intercedes for you, that day will find you ready and watching." That is, her prayers will win for us the grace of a happy death. Indeed, Newman even attributed the deathbed repentance of the Good Thief to the intercession of the Redeemer's mother standing below those three crosses in the Good Friday darkness.

Therefore we should not be fearful or anxious about our final moments. The operative virtue here is hope; it generates trust and confidence in the divine goodness and Mary's prayers, and expresses itself, in the case of God's holy ones, as "the confidence of a Christian with four aces," to quote Mark Twain. Thus Pauline Jaricot is on record as saying that she feared debt more than death. Pope John XXIII kept repeating on his deathbed: "How sweet it is to die for those who love the Lord's Sacred Heart." As for St. Theresa of Lisieux, she said simply that Jesus, not death, would come to take her to the world beyond.

The Evil of Evils

In the Church's prayer to St. Michael the Archangel, we ask him to defend and safeguard us against the devil's wickedness and snares; we also ask him to rebuke and cast down to hell "Satan and all wicked spirits who wander through the world for the ruin of souls."

Here the Church is focusing our faith on a reality that is all the more grim and threatening for being a revealed truth. Hordes of fallen angels are relentlesdly plotting our downfall, their intention being to lead us into that evil which surely out-evils all else---everlasting and irretrievable damnation in Hell.

Bear in mind that the mother of God has from the beginning been intimately involved in the unending struggle between good and evil, which in real terms is the struggle within human souls and for their winning. For she is the woman pitted in deadly enmity against God's enemy, the old serpent, as is her seed against his (cf. Gen 3: 15). Again, she is the woman clothed with the sun and locked in implacable conflict with the great red dragon (cf. Apoc 12: 11-18).

Clearly, then, we must stay close to Mary so as to enjoy maximum protection against her enemies and ours. Thus Fr William Faber's counsel applies to us all: "Devotion to Mary must grow until the hour when she will come to help us to die well, and so pass safely through the risk of doom."

Sunsets into Dawns

"Christ turns all our sunsets into dawns." Clement of Alexandria's saying can be applied very appropriately to the Lord's immaculate mother, whose eternal day dawned when she was assumed body and soul into Heaven. What this means is that, in recognition of and reward for her role as the New Eve and mother of the Redeemer, she was taken up with a glorified humanity into the City of God. And there our beautiful and loving mother acts as a sign of hope and comfort for her children still on their pilgrim way.

We therefore look to Mary as the bright dawn and exemplar of the brave new world God has ready for us beyond time's horizon. It is the world of the Beatific Vision and happiness without end, the world of transfigured human bodies endowed with resurrection radiance and unfading youth, the world of complete human fulfilment and perfect peace, the world of reunion forever with our much-missed dear ones.

Mother of the Millennium

Meanwhile we are still pilgrims and exiles as we plod our way day by day to that heavenly homeland, the City of Mary. And we do so as citizens of this brave old world of ours, which is so transitory and fragile, so full of sin and error, so bewildered and seductive. Yet it is nonetheless our God-given home, albeit an unabiding one, where we breathe his air and eat his bread, and wherein we can recognise the traces of his power, goodness and beauty in everything around us.

Towards this world we Christians have a double duty and responsibility. In the first place, as Vatican II has urged us, we must do all we can for its human advancement and material betterment, so that every man may live in conditions consonant with human dignity. And we shall continue to work towards this goal with all the more conviction and zeal because we are celebrating the arrival into it as a citizen 2000 years ago of the God-Man and Redeemer born of the Virgin Mary.

Our second Christian duty and responsibility towards our world is to do all we can and whenever we can to bring the truth and grace of the gospel into as many lives as possible. And here Mary, the Queen of Apostles, stands to help us mightily. Let us never forget that every single one of the six billion inhabitants of planet earth is for her a beloved son or daughter, a precious image of God, an immortal diamond destined to enjoy the Beatific Vision along with her for ever and ever.

Mary is therefore the morning star of our new millenium. We share the Holy Father's confidence that she who gave us the God-Man in the first place will bring signal blessings upon humanity at large as we celebrate his 2000th birthday. So we ask her, the Mother of Divine Grace and Mother of All Nations, to obtain for ourselves and our world a superabundance of grace for the hoped-for springtime of holiness and evangelization. And we make this request of her all the more confidently as we recall that momentous birth in the Bethlehem stable---"the place," said Chesterton, "where God was homeless and all men are at home."

Books Available by Fr. Richard Foley, SJ

MARY AND THE EUCHARIST
Foreword by Michael H. Brown
by FR. RICHARD FOLEY, SJ

Speaking out of profound study and wide personal and pastoral experience, Fr. Foley takes up, one after another, the challenging and comforting aspects of the Divine Relationship. The Eucharist is truly and really Jesus Christ. He insists on the Real Presence, as any faithful Catholic must. About it he raises so many illuminating and splendid subjects, all coming back to the Blessed Virgin Mary. ISBN: 1-891431-00-5, 198 pp.

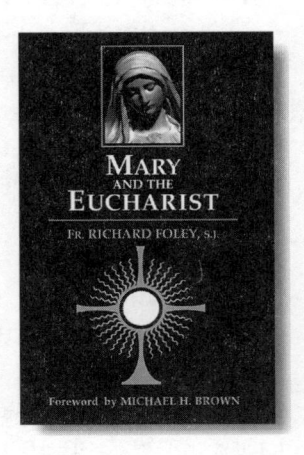

Only $10.95

THE DRAMA OF MEDJUGORJE
by FR. RICHARD FOLEY, SJ

In this book, Fr. Foley takes a deeper look into the great sacramental boom coming out of Medjugorje. The graces that have been given there are for the benefit of the world in the two decades immediately preceeding the third millennium. Learn about the final outcome of this great drama...eternal happiness in the next world.

ISBN: 1-85390-139-3, 158 pp.

Only $8.95

Toll-Free (888) 654-6279 or (412) 787-9735 www.SaintAndrew.com

Books by Dr. Thomas W. Petrisko

INSIDE HEAVEN AND HELL
What History, Theology, and the Mystics tell us about the Afterlife
by DR. THOMAS W. PETRISKO

Beginning with death and judgment, bestselling author Dr. Thomas Petrisko (*The Fatima Prophecies*) takes us on a spiritual journey with the saints, mystics, visionaries, and the Blessed Mother - inside Heaven and Hell. Will you be ready come Judgment Day? Discover what really happens at your judgment and how everything you say and do will be a cause for your eternal reward or, perhaps, your everlasting punishment. With profound new insight into what awaits each one of us, this book is a ***must read for all those who are serious about earning their 'salvation.'*** ISBN: 1-891903-23-3, 204 pp.

Only $12.95

IN GOD'S HANDS
The Miraculous Story of little Audrey Santo
by DR. THOMAS W. PETRISKO

The tragic victim of a drowning accident at age three, little Audrey Santo of Worcester, Ma. now lives confined to her bed. She has been in a coma-like state known as Akinetic Mutism for ten years. Yet, for some reason, God has taken her life and used it in a very special way. From the weeping statues that surround her, to what appears to be the Sacred Stigmata, to claims of prayers miraculously answered through Audrey's reported intercession, this silent, suffering child has become a testimony of life in a culture of death. Audrey's story has received national media and was featured on **ABC's 20/20**. ***BESTSELLER!*** ISBN: 1-891903-04-7, 234 pp.

Only $12.95

Toll-Free (888) 654-6279 or (412) 787-9735 www.SaintAndrew.com

Books Available by Dr. Thomas W. Petrisko

THE FATIMA PROPHECIES
At the Doorstep of the World
by DR. THOMAS W. PETRISKO

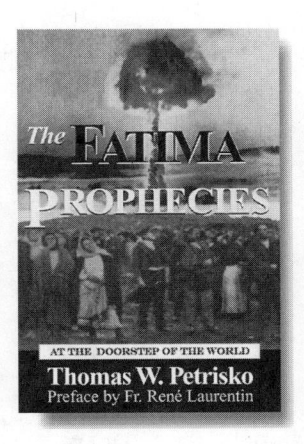

Beginning approximately ten years before the French Revolution, Dr. Thomas Petrisko takes a look at the hundreds of apparitions and miracles that occurred in the nineteenth century all the way up until the apparitions at Fatima in 1917. He then confronts the rise of Communism and nuclear warfare in association with the two unfulfilled prophecies of Fatima: the annihilation of nations and the Triumph of the Immaculate Heart and Era of Peace. Written in a fast moving, popular style, this book also tells of the many contemporary prophecies and apparitions and how they point to the fulfillment of Fatima. **BESTSELLER!** ISBN: 1-891903-06-3, 486 pp.

Only $14.95

THE KINGDOM OF OUR FATHER
Who is God the Father?
by DR. THOMAS W. PETRISKO

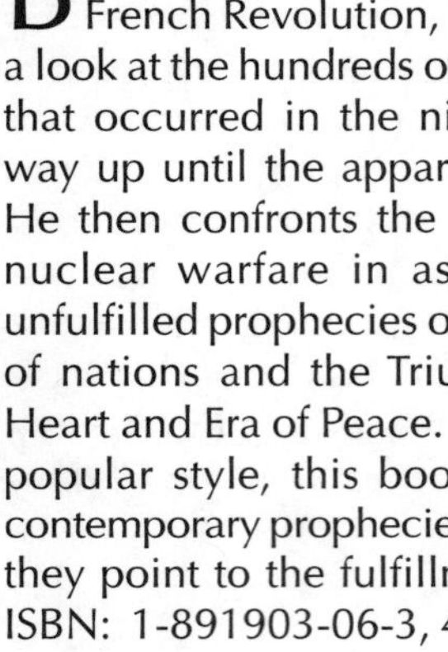

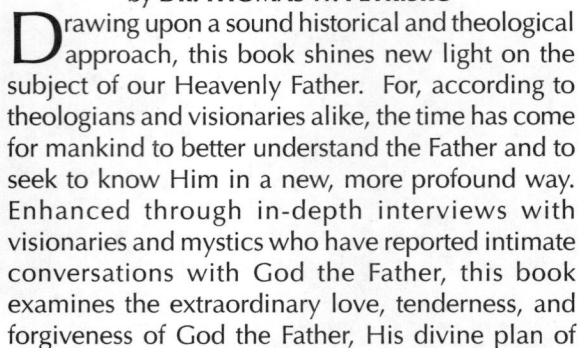

Drawing upon a sound historical and theological approach, this book shines new light on the subject of our Heavenly Father. For, according to theologians and visionaries alike, the time has come for mankind to better understand the Father and to seek to know Him in a new, more profound way. Enhanced through in-depth interviews with visionaries and mystics who have reported intimate conversations with God the Father, this book examines the extraordinary love, tenderness, and forgiveness of God the Father, His divine plan of mercy for the world at this time, and the prophesied coming of His Kingdom in the new Millennium. ISBN: 1-891903-18-7, 356 pp.

Only $14.95

Toll-Free (888) 654-6279 or (412) 787-9735 www.SaintAndrew.com